THE SEL COACH

THE SEL COACH

Planning and Implementation Resources for Social Emotional Learning Leaders

Jennifer E. Rogers

FOR INFORMATION:

Corwin
A SAGE Company
2455 Teller Road
Thousand Oaks, California 91320
(800) 233-9936
www.corwin.com

SAGE Publications Ltd.
1 Oliver's Yard
55 City Road
London EC1Y 1SP
United Kingdom

SAGE Publications India Pvt. Ltd.
B 1/I 1 Mohan Cooperative Industrial Area
Mathura Road, New Delhi 110 044
India

SAGE Publications Asia-Pacific Pte. Ltd.
18 Cross Street #10-10/11/12
China Square Central
Singapore 048423

President: Mike Soules
Vice President and
  Editorial Director: Monica Eckman
Publisher: Jessica Allan
Content Development
  Editor: Mia Rodriguez
Editorial Assistant: Natalie Delpino
Copy Editor: Integra
Typesetter: C&M Digitals (P) Ltd.
Proofreader: Lawrence W. Baker
Cover Designer: Gail Buschman
Marketing Manager: Olivia Bartlett

Printed in the United States of America

Library of Congress Cataloging-in-Publication Data

Names: Rogers, Jennifer E., author.

Title: The SEL coach : planning and implementation resources for social emotional learning leaders / Jennifer E. Rogers.

Description: Thousand Oaks, California : Corwin, 2023. | Includes bibliographical references and index.

Identifiers: LCCN 2021063122 | ISBN 9781071870914 (paperback) | ISBN 9781071870921 (epub) | ISBN 9781071870938 (epub) | ISBN 9781071870945 (pdf)

Subjects: LCSH: Affective education—United States. | Mentoring in education—United States. | Teachers—In-service training—United States. | Educational change—United States.

Classification: LCC LB1072 .R663 2022 | DDC 370.15/340973—dc23/eng/20220217
LC record available at https://lccn.loc.gov/2021063122

This book is printed on acid-free paper.

22 23 24 25 26 10 9 8 7 6 5 4 3 2 1

CONTENTS

PREFACE

To Superintendents and District/Building Administrators

While much of this book is dedicated to the individuals who are considered Social Emotional Learning (SEL) coaches or lead implementers, leaders of districts are a vitally important part of any system change effort. Your support through time, budget, and advocating for the importance of developing social and emotional competencies is crucial. SEL has been around for over 25 years. Its importance in developing youth who can build relationships, make informed decisions, and use problem-solving skills has been validated through countless research articles and publications. These evidence-based outcomes of the benefits for students and adults to have social and emotional competencies help to produce productive citizens.

A recent study found that there have been significant effects on youth well-being after the pandemic. Speaking to educators nationwide, they have talked about not only the academic lag that some students have experienced but also their social and emotional competencies. This looks like more fighting, more disconnection from school and classmates, stress reactions, referrals to the counselor, and absenteeism. While it will be some time before we get more comprehensive data on the effects of the pandemic, school leaders are reporting the changes they see from before March 2020 until now. The August 2021 report "How Has the Pandemic Affected Students' Social-Emotional Well-Being? A Review of the Evidence to Date" found the following:

- A significant portion of young people, likely 30–40%, have experienced negative impacts on their mental or social-emotional health during the pandemic.

- Students who learned remotely for long periods of time and historically marginalized students were more likely to experience these negative effects.

- Rates of anxiety and attempted suicides, already on the rise pre-pandemic, appear to have increased among all students, especially among girls.

- While some students fared well initially or even fared better when learning remotely than they did in person before the pandemic, these positive effects did not last. Negative effects for students increased over time.

- Schools and districts, especially in rural areas without a strong social service infrastructure, lacked systems to track student well-being or strategies to address and improve it (Hamilton et al., 2021, p. 6).

You may be aware of why SEL is important and how it can mediate some of the effects of social isolation and the stress of the pandemic. But I would like to invite you to consider how funding an SEL coach or lead implementer can magnify your efforts.

WHY AN SEL COACH?

The Social Emotional Learning coach is a relatively new position. There are districts across the country that have begun to find it necessary to create this position to help organize the people, resources, and tasks that must take place for SEL implementation.

SEL coaches can come from a variety of places within the system. They can be school counselors, psychologists, teachers, administrators, social workers, and the like. They can have the role of SEL exclusively or as a part of another role. It does not necessarily matter what role they have been in previously. What matters is the skill sets that they have or can develop in the service of this work. One of those things is the ability to demonstrate these competencies in difficult and demanding settings.

Schools need SEL coaches or lead implementers to effectively support the heavy lift of systems change. Individuals with the expertise and training can help to solve the unique challenges that SEL implementation creates in individual systems. School leaders start with good intentions but lack the time, resources, and expertise to create system change without someone who can provide them with the support to implement schoolwide SEL. Therefore, an SEL coach can be a game changer.

An SEL coach can help administrators during the implementation process. "Principals experience substantial job-related stress, yet they often lack the guidance and resources necessary to develop their own social and emotional competencies (SECs) that could help them respond appropriately. A large proportion of principals feel that they lack the requisite skills to effectively lead their schools, and high turnover rates create a significant financial and operational burden" (Mahfouz et al., 2019, p. 3). In many communities, understanding how to select and integrate intentional supports that help staff deal with the uncertainty of starting something new and complex is a barrier to SEL implementation. The skills that educational stakeholders need to effectively manage an SEL implementation are not currently taught in many preservice or higher education training programs. Effective SEL coaches should have the ability to lead, have strong communication skills, provide data support, conduct professional development and training for other adults, coach throughout the system, and team with educational stakeholders and community members. The SEL coach can be the lever to transform an idea into an action plan and goals into outcomes.

SEL coaches focus on creating a productive environment. This person needs to keep many different things in mind while providing coaching. They are monitoring the entire system to determine the focus of their practice. An SEL coach may be working with the administration to create equitable discipline procedures. They may work with individual teachers to integrate Social Emotional Learning curriculum into the teaching day. The SEL coach may do observations for students to try and determine the antecedent of a behavior. The SEL coach may work with parents to educate them on the skills that are being taught at school so they may have a common language at home. The SEL coach may work with the bus drivers to give them strategies they can use to communicate with students that provide a good entry to school. We choose to implement social and emotional learning to impact student outcomes. But students learn best when they see these competencies practiced and modeled by the adults around them. And that is where the SEL coach can make a huge difference in promoting, teaching, leading, communicating, and supporting all educational stakeholders in demonstrating these valuable skills.

WHO CAN BE AN SEL COACH? QUALIFICATIONS

SEL coach skill sets include the ability to collaborate and work together for a common good—the ability to have difficult conversations, which means to come up with multiple solutions to problems, reflect on the perspectives of others, focus on the big picture, and not get stuck on the small stuff. This will require the ability to mediate or compromise when stuck on a specific issue. And this may also involve knowing when to get the administration to the table to figure out really challenging situations. Of course, being able to problem-solve will be necessary. Problem-solving includes defining the problem, determining the cause of the problem, creating and prioritizing solutions and alternatives, and then implementing the best probable solution. SEL coaches need to be able to manage their time well. And this includes scheduling and managing time for self and others. Power struggles can occur in the school environment. The coach will need to be adept at dealing with them by listening and validating the experiences of others. Another quality is to be a flexible thinker. This is the ability to shift thinking or attention in response to the unexpected or new, such as a new mandate or district focus that may add complications to their current work with SEL. In essence, the ideal SEL coach has the willingness and capacity to embody and model SEL skills with other educational stakeholders.

Potential Job Description

The ideal candidate's professional background includes the following:

1. Time in the classroom: teaching, subbing, working as paraprofessional in desired grade level: elementary, middle, and high

2. Education in school counseling, mental health/community counseling, special education, school psychology, social work, instructional coaching, behavior support

3. Previous exposure to SEL, MTSS, PBIS, or RTI: understands the basics of system change

4. Professional growth habits: new certification, trainings, and continued pursuit of knowledge

5. Experience delivering and creating professional development

6. Previous experience with SEL curriculum and competencies

How Can Leadership Assist in the Development of SEL Coaches in the System?

While hiring an SEL coach will help your school community build and strengthen their SEL foundation, it is important to remember that there are some additional elements to make this position successful. To be successful, their relationship with your school system must start positively. There are a few essential components that should be in place to give SEL coaches the foundation to start their work. Initially, coaches need an induction or onboarding process, an action plan, and professional development.

Induction/Onboarding Process

The first thing that SEL coaches need is an induction or onboarding process. Induction programs are comprehensive systems of support that help bridge the preservice to service development of beginning educators. Induction programs address both the practical needs of beginning coaches (who, what, when, and why) and nurture coach professional development (the how). Onboarding programs are important for the SEL leader, and the school community. This is also an ideal time to observe the school community and begin building positive relationships with the people in the system. During the onboarding process, the SEL coach will begin building relationships with teachers and principals. They will also identify key members of the school community, especially those who could support implementation. This includes implementation leaders, other coaches, and resource managers. Who is critical to the position's success? Who will be a strong partner? The SEL coach will need to meet those individuals quickly and establish a positive rapport. The SEL coach will also benefit from understanding the particular practices within your specific school environment.

Creating an Action Plan

An action plan will need to be determined by school leadership for the SEL coach to begin their new learning. These are some introductory steps for the first few weeks of school.

SAMPLE: Action Plan

- Introductions to key building leadership

- A brief overview of the hierarchical structure of your school or district

- Understand previous experience with SEL: Ask about positive and negative and what worked and didn't work

- Give information to the SEL coach about the history and need for the SEL coach role

- Establish the coach role with the school or district: include establishing dos and don'ts for the role

- Develop a document for the role of coaches for dissemination to faculty

- Set expectations for the SEL coach role including primary and secondary roles and assignments
  - Primary assignments: Leader of implementation at school level, training, coaching, professional development, data support, team member, communicator
  - Secondary assignments include meetings, webpage, parent night organization, training, engagement, community outreach, resource manager

- Set up a meeting with principals
  - Prepare with questions and discussion topics
  - Questions about role
  - Topics could include
    - Team structure
    - Meeting schedule
    - Office space/work schedule
    - Staff PD/introduction
    - Action plan (for both the year and first few weeks)

A continued emphasis on growing skill sets for the SEL coach will provide educators with tools to grow and expand their skills. Additional training is extremely beneficial for all new staff. Training should be focused on providing meaningful experiences for the SEL coach. Professional development can include conferences, professional speakers, or authors related to a specific area of education and SEL.

SAMPLE: Training and Resources for SEL Coach Role

- Invest in additional technical training and resources/Build coach capacity
- Additional technical training for the coach role
  - Computer systems: internal
  - Excel
  - OneNote, Google Docs, or other shared data collection
  - Website creation/maintenance
- Data collection and analysis
- Communication skills
- How to lead meetings and create agendas
- Resources
  - Access to articles, websites, internet
  - Books
  - Outside trainings
- Make forms consistent for all coaches
  - Such as:
    - Inventory of programs and initiatives
    - Action planning
    - Intervention tracking form
    - Task list
    - Tiered fidelity inventory

SAMPLE: Agenda for Two-Day Training for Coaches at Beginning of Year

- Day 1:
  - Introductions and Icebreakers
  - Discussion: Things I am looking forward to in this role; questions or concerns I have about the role
  - Job description
  - Assign mentors (if available)
  - Create norms for meetings
  - Highlights of last year
  - Strategies for coaching
- Day 2:
  - Tiered fidelity inventory
  - Year at a glance
  - Organizing a typical day
  - Specific content training
  - Using data for effectiveness and efficiency
  - Self-care strategies

Training Schedule (example)

Training for SEL Coach: Phase One

DATE	TRAINING	DELIVERED BY	RESOURCES	AREA OF FOCUS

(Continued)

(Continued)

DATE	TRAINING	DELIVERED BY	RESOURCES	AREA OF FOCUS

As the superintendent or district/building leader, these are some suggestions to ease the transition of this new role in your system. As with any new role, there will need to be grace for the growing pains. But supporting the SEL coach role will allow for your SEL implementation to flourish.

PREFACE
To the SEL Coach

Whether you have been in the role of SEL coach for a while or whether you are brand-new to the position, the intent of this book is to provide you with resources and ideas for moving your SEL implementation to the next level. SEL coaches come from various backgrounds and experiences. To understand and identify with the teachers and students you work with, it is important to draw from your own previous experiences. This will help to develop empathy between you and others. Use your past work and personal experiences not only to identify effective models of systems change but also to connect with those you are collaborating with. Be open and honest with others as you continue to work on these competencies and qualities.

Being in the role of SEL coach or SEL lead implementer can be a challenge with very few resources to help you on your journey. You may be wondering how to be an SEL coach or what should a lead implementer do? This also may be your only role or a role that you do in combination with other roles. As you will learn in this book, the SEL coach/lead implementer (which will be shortened to SEL coach) is most like a systems coach. Because social and emotional competencies affect everyone in the system, a coach is there to guide all educational stakeholders in practices that support these skills. For example, for a student to learn how to manage their stress, they should be taught how to do it. But learning does not stop there, it should then be practiced with other peers and adults. And then adults should be able to model stress management. We should also be able to support each other in managing our stress, if needed, through social support. There are individual, group, and systemic elements to mastering this skill. The SEL coach would identify areas of need and work with the students and adults to develop solutions to systemic problems. "System coaching can include coaching at the individual, small group, and organizational levels, depending upon the need and level of the educational organization. Further, systems coaching activities can include those activities in which educators with content knowledge expertise provide support directly to teachers for instructional design and delivery to students" (March & Gaunt, 2013, p. 3).

In addition to coaching competencies, it is also important to be aware of the coaching qualities needed to be a successful coach. Being an SEL leader means being knowledgeable in multiple areas to ensure the best chance of choosing the right implementation for your system. Coaching has been a part of the educational system for years. There are many individuals who describe the competencies that a coach must possess. The one that is most applicable and provides a systems-level view is identified by Zins and Erchul (2002). The competencies include self-awareness or the awareness of one's interpersonal style. This is critical when approaching someone as a coach. Self-awareness allows for the understanding of one's assets and challenges. This includes qualities such as good interpersonal skills; knowledge of intervention technology (content expertise); understanding of the influence of school climate, norms, and values on the coaching process; and sensitivity to cultural diversity and awareness of sociocultural factors (Zins & Erchul, 2002).

QUALITIES OF A COACH

1. Demonstrates knowledge of core concepts (teachers can be a tough audience: need to know that you know something due to experience, intensive knowledge that can add value to their work)

2. Demonstrates flexibility and collaboration working with a team

3. Understands and can apply that knowledge of theory into practices

4. Possesses knowledge of state and federal laws

5. Has an understanding of the roles/responsibilities of staff in the school environment

6. Has the ability to adapt to different leadership styles and build relationships with principals and staff

7. Has the ability to collect and interpret data to inform systems change

Each SEL coach's experience will be different. Just like the unique environments you will be working in, your role may look different than other SEL coaches. The purpose of this book is for you to have many different practices and processes for you to use that will help your system implement SEL effectively. The information and exercises provided here will give you tools to navigate your unique community and role within it to provide solutions that will meet your specific needs. The purpose of this book is to support you in your role as an SEL coach by giving you practices and processes to try in your unique school culture.

BEGINNING STEPS: TO-DO CHECKLIST

You may want to know, what should I do RIGHT NOW. This list is to help you with some ideas to start the activities and practices of being an SEL coach before getting too deep into the book. Here is a list of ideas to begin your journey as an SEL coach.

SEL Coach To-Do List: Where to Start

- [ ] Introduce self to school: include roles, responsibilities, and contact information
- [ ] Set up a regular meeting with the principal and appropriate administration (weekly or biweekly)
- [ ] Connect with staff
  - Attend grade-level or subject team meetings
  - In the staff break room
  - At out-of-school activities
  - Meet and greet new staff members personally
- [ ] Plan schedule
- [ ] Plan for options for PD with teachers
- [ ] Make schedule public
- [ ] Create coaching log
- [ ] Find ways to be invited into the classroom
  - Talk to staff about common problems
  - Listen to them
  - Offer a collaboration time sign-up
  - Go in with staff members with whom you already have a relationship
  - Email staff to offer support
- [ ] Create or meet with the SEL team and add new members if necessary
- [ ] Update your contact information on any websites with new job responsibilities
- [ ] Schedule any planned PD for the year
- [ ] Determine data collection plan
- [ ] Begin self-care planning for staff
- [ ] Review available resources and materials
- [ ] Connect to all tech sources used by the building
- [ ] Consider optimal communications with other stakeholders: email, newsletters, etc.

PUBLISHER'S ACKNOWLEDGMENTS

Corwin gratefully acknowledges the contributions of the following reviewers:

Elizabeth Alvarez
Superintendent of Schools
Forest Park School District 91
Forest Park, IL

Allison Hancock
Social Emotional Behavior Coach
St. Mary's County Public Schools
Leonardtown, MD

Miriam Ojaghi
SEL and Middle School Consultant
DeKalb Regional Office of Education
DeKalb, IL

ABOUT THE AUTHOR

Jennifer Rogers is founder of Rogers Training Solutions, LLC. She works with educational stakeholders on developing tools and strategies to increase positive student outcomes. Rogers Training Solutions, LLC provides consulting, professional development, workshops, coaching, and one-on-one leadership support for individuals and organizations exploring social, emotional, and behavioral interventions in school environments.

Dr. Rogers's background has reflected a strong commitment to children and adolescents and their families for over 20 years. She is proud to work side by side with educators in promoting social and emotional competencies for all students. She has worked with school districts across the country as a school counselor, researcher, district administrator, coach trainer, and consultant. Schools benefit from her experience as a licensed professional counselor (LPC) and training as a counselor educator to create programs to meet the social, emotional, and behavioral needs of students.

She has experience with implementing and measuring the impact of interventions in counseling, prevention, and early intervention. She has advocated for, written about, researched, trained, created interventions for, used data to support, worked with curriculum, and implemented districtwide Social Emotional Learning. Her book *Leading for Change Through Whole-School Social Emotional Learning: Strategies to Build a Positive School Culture* (2019) has been adopted by educators and is currently being used in multiple districts. She trains educators in best practices to meet the needs of their specific culture and students.

Dr. Rogers's professional goals align with the core mission to make social and emotional learning an integral part of education for all students. To reach the goal, she believes that we must work to support the educators through systemic change and create a common understanding amongst all stakeholders of the benefits of Social Emotional Learning to positive school culture.

CHAPTER 1

....

THE SOCIAL EMOTIONAL LEARNING COACH ROLE

SEL COACH ROLES AND RESPONSIBILITIES: DEFINITIONS

As a Social Emotional Learning (SEL) coach, you will serve in many roles within the school community. It is important to not only understand the different roles you play but also explore what they mean to you. The clarity that you can provide will be crucial for yourself and the stakeholders. If you can define what these responsibilities entail, you can explain them to others. This will in turn be helpful in illuminating what your role as an SEL coach is and what is not.

EXERCISE: Define what these roles mean to you as an SEL coach

Facilitator:

_____

_____

SEL team member/team lead:

_____

_____

(Continued)

(Continued)

Direct coaching:

_____

_____

Professional development/trainer:

_____

_____

Data collector:

_____

_____

Communicator:

_____

_____

DEFINITION OF ROLES

Leader/Facilitator

As a leader or facilitator, the role of an SEL coach is to build a foundation to support the implementation. Developing collaborative relationships is important and requires trust and understanding as you develop partnerships with educational stakeholders. As part of this work, your role is to be the "face" of the SEL implementation.

- Build a foundation and vision through collaboration with stakeholders.
- Develop goals in collaboration with stakeholders.
- Influence school culture in a positive way.
- Commit to equity.
- Build relationships with stakeholders, teachers, and staff.

- Promote understanding of SEL.
- Positively report and promote the progress being made by students, staff, and the community as it relates to your endeavors.

Coaching

Being an effective coach can only occur when you have a high level of trust within the school community. Once those in the community trust you, they will be more open to listening to your recommendations. Your coaching role is both collaborative and innovative. As a coach, you will work directly with staff to ensure that teachers and administrators have the support they need to implement successful SEL practices and interventions. One of your primary goals will be to help educational stakeholders learn and be able to effectively implement SEL practices and interventions. As a coach, it's important to teach and model effective practices that teachers can use in their classrooms, using varied techniques to coach based on individual needs. Then you can informally observe teachers as they try them out and offer positive and adjusting feedback on how to increase the effectiveness of their SEL implementation.

- Work directly with staff to implement interventions and teach the selected program.
- Understand and teach prevention (universal) work as the foundation.
- Use different modalities to coach staff based on their needs.
- Discover procedures to access individuals who may need help.
- Acknowledge positive practices of staff and students and celebrate accomplishments.

Data Support/Collection

Prior to implementing specific models of change, it is important to become efficient in data collection and support. Identifying and collecting current SEL behavior and academic data within your school community will provide you with a clear view of the needs of both teachers and students. The data you collect will give you the opportunity to identify gaps within the system that may be preventing them from achieving their goals. Once you have implemented an SEL initiative, monitoring growth is critical. SEL measurement data provides leaders, teachers, and students with insights on SEL skills and helps to identify areas of improvement. First determine what data you need to collect, and then monitor each data point to measure each to determine the effectiveness of your initiatives. To improve outcomes for students, schools must strategically measure and monitor the progress of their SEL curriculum implementation. How will you know if students' SEL skills are improving? One way to collect data is to survey your students, staff, and families several times per year to assess the effectiveness of the SEL practices your school is using.

- Identify and collect current data.

- Identify gaps and encourage new ways of gaining missing data.

- Focus on data to support student outcomes.

- Monitor progress to aid in the decision-making process.

- Help in the implementation of screening and assessment measures.

- Develop plans for results of data.

- Conduct periodic surveys of staff and students to gauge effectiveness.

Professional Development/Trainer

As the SEL coach, you'll likely have opportunities to lead professional development sessions and train your educational stakeholders on effective SEL practices. As a part of your sessions, you'll create awareness and understanding of core SEL concepts. You will want to model different learning modalities to keep your audience engaged. You'll share evidence-based SEL practices and empower your staff by including their voices in the process.

- Create awareness and understanding of concepts.

- Use multiple modalities to engage the audience.

- Inform staff of evidence-based practices.

- Engage staff in learning and advocating for their needs in the process.

Communicator

Working collaboratively with others requires effective communication skills. As an effective communicator, you will work with educators and administrators to share practices and keep all educational stakeholders informed about SEL implementation. Actively listening and being open to feedback will act as a demonstration of modeling these behaviors to the educational community.

- Share practices used by different stakeholders throughout the system.

- Develop the ability to listen actively, summarize, and make actionable the things that are needed by the stakeholders.

- Work in collaborative relationships with different individuals and teams.

- Advocate for the needs of the program and process.

- Model effective interpersonal communication skills.

Teaming/Member or Lead

When you work with others in the school community, remember that you are a part of a team. As you approach teachers and administrators, be sure to cultivate an environment that is both welcoming and supportive. This will establish better relationships and allow you to be more effective. Creating this type of environment will also help to gain team member commitment. Establishing yourself as a supportive colleague and team member will help you build stronger relationships and allow you to be more effective. This environment will also help to increase the investment of your team.

- Establish commitment of team members at school.

- Facilitate data-based decision-making process.

- Create an environment that is both supportive and focused on achieving goals.

- Use organizational tools to further work.

- Empower educators to lead SEL implementation together.

SEL COACHING COMPETENCIES

As an SEL coach, there are critical competencies that you will need to develop to be successful. Each one provides you with an additional way of working with people effectively. It will also help to develop a sensitivity to your school community. These competencies include self-awareness, strong interpersonal skills, knowledge of various intervention technologies, understanding of the influence of school culture and climate, and a sensitivity to cultural diversity. Your work as an SEL coach will require you to consider the entire school when choosing models to implement. These competencies support a mindset that will make you more effective and prepared to meet the needs of your educational stakeholders.

Leaders build the foundation and relationships with others. As an SEL coach, the collaborative relationships you create will lead to trust and understanding as well. You will work directly with educational partners in your school community. This work will develop goals for the educational stakeholders and the school system.

When implementing any kind of change, there are the actions or activities to promote change (way of doing) and the process of how change occurs (way of being). You can have the practices but not the mindset or the mindset change with no practices. But the best interventions have both practices, which are a series of actions to achieve a particular result and the process of how change occurs. The SEL coach will need to have both the way of doing and the way of being. The SEL coach will need to have practices and processes in their toolkit. Your role is to support social and emotional competencies. This includes the practices of intervention, curricula, lesson plans, techniques, checklists, and rubrics. Processes involve mindset, discussion, reflection, beliefs, and motivation. While practices can often be seen and checked off a to-do list, processes are how real change happens through thinking and considering making changes that will further develop the educator's ability to meet students where they are and promote positive growth in social and emotional competence. One of the first tasks is to build a change-agent mindset.

MANAGING UNCERTAINTY BY ADOPTING A CHANGE-AGENT MINDSET

Stress can be caused by uncertainty and unpredictability. When learning and teaching new practices, it can cause a lot of discomfort. One coach reported, "I'm still managing my discomfort in terms of not yet having a very clear sense of the direction of my school. There's a lot to take in these first two weeks with getting my schedule established, getting to know staff and students, having a solid understanding of my role, and getting more comfortable with it. Learning the dynamics in the building is helping me to know what sorts of questions to ask when I'm meeting with staff. These initial conversations have been very insightful! But because of all of this, my excitement for the work comes and goes. However, some days I feel so overwhelmed and anxious. But I know that will ease with time, it just sucks when you're in the middle of it. I just wonder if I'm 'on the right track' and I'm nervous that there's something I'm supposed to be doing that has completely fallen off my radar." It is important to normalize these feelings in a new role.

How Will You Manage Uncertainty in Your Role? Who Will Support You?

As the SEL coach, you will make a significant impact on the educational stakeholders in your school community. Your leadership is necessary but not sufficient for moving forward with positive school culture. I discuss the impact that the change agent (you) can make in *Leading for Change Through Whole School Social Emotional Learning: Strategies to Build a Positive School Culture* (Rogers, 2019). That book is a great introduction to strategies for systemic change through Social Emotional Learning. In this current book, you will learn more strategies and tools for the change agent. And as the SEL coach, it is important to recognize that there are some mindsets that will be crucial to your overall success. They include being a big picture thinker, always in a learning stance, being the keeper of the vision, asking questions, having tools and strategies, being open to different voices, having the ability to direct or redirect the work, being able to have multiple concepts in flux, and having a network of support. Two additional qualities that change agents should have are valuing their work and trusting themselves and the process.

PREVIOUS EXPERIENCE/LOOKING FORWARD

It may be helpful to ask yourself what experiences you have had previously that can be useful in the role of SEL coach. This process of reflection is recommended throughout your new learning. Answer the questions below about your previous experience in education and considerations for problem-solving common issues.

Coach reflections: Previous experience/looking forward

1. Detail the previous experience you have had with SEL or any other schoolwide social emotional or behavioral programs. How long were you a part of it? What was your role?

2. What did you find was most effective about the program?

3. What did you find did not work during the program implementation?

4. What is the best way to increase schoolwide implementation of social emotional learning in your experience?

5. What are you looking forward to in your role as SEL coach or lead implementer?

6. What questions or concerns do you have about your role as the SEL coach or lead implementer?

7. As a coach/lead implementer, you will be responsible for planning and leading training with adult learners. What are two or three things you always consider when planning training for adults?

8. In coaching teachers at a school, what are the most important messages you would give to teachers regarding relationships with students?

9. What three qualities do you value most in an educator?

10. How would you coach a teacher who thus far has not been willing to utilize SEL in their classroom?

11. One of the teachers you work with has asked you to remove a disruptive student from a teacher's class for several consecutive days. How do you respond and what are your next steps?

12. What is your experience with communicating with educational stakeholders? What have you found to be most effective in your communications?

CHAPTER 2

·····························

INTEGRATING
AN SEL COACH
IN YOUR SYSTEM

ANOTHER COACH? WHY SEL COACHES WHO
FOCUS ON WHOLE SCHOOL SEL ARE NECESSARY

As you will learn in this book, the SEL coach/lead implementer is most like a systems coach. Because social and emotional competencies affect everyone in the system, a coach is there to guide all educational stakeholders in practices that support these skills. It is important to provide clarity for your role: What makes the SEL coach different, similar, and vital for Social Emotional Learning success?

SEL coaches collaborate with colleagues to identify areas of need and develop systemic solutions. The word *coach* is defined as a person involved in the direction, instruction, and training of the operations of a team or of individual people. A coach may also be a teacher. An SEL coach has the additional responsibility of moving a system. Systems change takes a broader view to determining what changes can be made to impact our day-to-day lives in a positive way. With a systems mindset, the SEL coach looks at individual, group, whole school, and community influences particularly as they relate to social and emotional competencies. This may mean looking at a particular policy that negatively affects the school environment, or practices within the classroom, or the way an individual can effectively emotionally regulate. You will look at curricula and practices with an eye on how they will affect the system as well as individuals. You will not only look at the specific practices of individuals but also how those practices impact the rest of the system, especially the students.

SEL Coach versus Instructional Coach

Though SEL and instructional coaches have some similarities, it is important to understand what makes these roles different. Instructional coaches focus on the teaching and learning aspects of teacher performance and improvement. Areas such as student achievement and learning targets are their key areas of concentration. By comparison, SEL coaches focus on schoolwide efforts to improve the positive cultures of both school and classroom environments. The goals you set are designed to affect the overall well-being of both students and adults. This includes working with teachers, administrators, students, and families. Both instructional and SEL coaches benefit schools, increase efficiency, and contribute to creating a positive culture.

Instructional coaches often focus on student achievement. System coaches focus on creating a productive environment. The instructional coach can rely on specific learning targets, the students can be regularly assessed, and the coach and teacher can determine what type of instruction can meet the individual student needs (Sweeney, 2011). System coaches need to keep many different things in mind while providing coaching. They are monitoring the entire system to determine the focus of their practice. "The role of change coaching does not necessarily exclude direct work with teachers or an interest in classroom instruction, but rather understands classroom instruction as one piece of a larger systemic unit requiring change. This change coaches work with district and school leadership to build capacity of the system to support and evolving professional environment toward enhanced student outcomes" (March & Gaunt, 2013, p. 6).

SEL COACH VERSUS INSTRUCTIONAL COACH

Similarities

- Focus on instructional practice that effectively meets the needs of their specific students
- Not evaluative
- Use student evidence to make informed decisions
- Partner with leadership and teachers

Differences

- Instructional coaches are driven by student-learning goals
- Instructional coaches use state mandated standards-based learning targets, but SEL standards are not mandated in every state
- SEL coaches partner with every educational stakeholder in and outside the school environment

SEL Coach versus PBIS Coach

When comparing SEL and behavior or PBIS coaches, SEL coaches focus on enhancing the social and emotional well-being of all stakeholders through curricula, practices, and schoolwide systems. They implement SEL strategies with both students and adults, including both staff and families. SEL coaches target developing lifelong social and emotional competencies in the classrooms and all corners of the campus. Behavior or PBIS coaches are typically responsible for schoolwide behavior and discipline data collection, focusing specifically on behavior and discipline. They also set and teach behavioral expectations and acknowledge students for meeting these expectations. Both SEL and behavior coaches promote positive skills and environments rather than punitive or exclusionary discipline. They both also promote interventions at all tiers and expand and sustain the implementation of programs and interventions throughout their school or district.

SEL COACH VERSUS PBIS COACH

Similarities

- Expand and sustain implementation throughout the school or district
- Use data to guide direction of the work
- Use interventions at Tier 1, Tier 2, and Tier 3 levels
- Facilitate team meetings

Differences

- PBIS coaches are responsible for specific schoolwide data collection methods
- PBIS coaches work with discipline procedures and data including defining majors and minors in the system
- PBIS coaches are responsible for creating expectations, celebrations, reteaching opportunities, and reinforcement methods

SEL Coach versus MTSS Coach

SEL and MTSS, or multitiered systems of support, coaches align in several very important areas including promoting equity and taking specific needs into account. The motivations behind the two roles are slightly different. While MTSS coaches focus on specific achievement objectives, SEL leaders factor in environment, climate, and culture to promote better behaviors that lead to higher achievement. The driving force is implementing strong social and emotional initiatives to help students and adults acquire and effectively apply the knowledge, attitudes, and skills necessary to understand and manage emotions, set and achieve positive goals, feel and show empathy for others, establish and maintain positive relationships, and make responsible decisions.

Similarities

- Promote equity for all students in the learning environment
- Invest in understanding systems that impact our students and staff
- Provide feedback on the fidelity of interventions
- Use problem-solving processes that consider unique needs of school or system

Differences

- MTSS coaches focus on closing the achievement gaps
- MTSS coaches use a variety of assessment strategies to determine academic needs
- MTSS coaches use multiple sources of data to improve teaching and learning

SEL Coach versus Sports Coach

Another form of coaching in schools is sports coaching. Though these two positions may not appear to be similar, there are some overlapping components. Both groups provide encouragement to students and understand the concept of motivation. Your role, however, will be to motivate teachers and students to create more productive and positive environments. Remember that in many positions within the system, there will be some overlap. You will work as a team to make things better throughout the school system.

SEL COACH VERSUS SPORTS COACH

Similarities

- Provide encouragement to stakeholders
- Understand motivation
- Understood to have multiple tools at disposal to use in different circumstances
- Create different strategies for different circumstances

Differences

- Sports coaches work mostly with students only
- Sports coaches may still use punishment for not accomplishing goals
- Sports coaches have more intensive time to focus on specific skills

COLLABORATION WITH ROLES IN YOUR SYSTEM

As you begin to communicate your multiple roles and responsibilities in the system, it might help to develop a visual like the one below. The purpose is to demonstrate some of the collaborative work that can be shared between these roles. Creating a collaboration visual can help educational stakeholders better understand how they can work with the SEL coach. The purpose is to provide as much clarity as possible and give the other stakeholders a road-map for contact points between the different roles.

WHAT IF SEL COACH IS NOT YOUR ONLY ROLE?

Your school may be fortunate enough to include multiple layers of a hierarchy that include a director of SEL, SEL coordinator, SEL coach, and other specialized roles. Or you may be the only one in your system responsible for SEL, but it is your full-time job. Or you may have another role in your system, and you are adding or have been asked to perform the role of SEL coach alongside your current role. The roles and responsibilities that are contained in this chapter may be spread over a few different people or it may be all in one person.

As an SEL coach or a lead implementer, you will serve many roles within your school community. It is not only important to understand the different roles that you play but how these roles overlap—specifically, how they relate in a multitiered system of support. It may be helpful to create a graphic that looks at how the different parts of your roles interact and intersect. It will help the educational stakeholders to understand what the combination of roles means for them.

THE IMPORTANT RELATIONSHIP BETWEEN
SEL COACH AND ADMINISTRATION/PRINCIPALS

Principals are under a tremendous amount of pressure. They are responsible for the difficult task of meeting the needs of several stakeholders while keeping the academic achievement of students top of mind. There is a cycle that occurs too frequently in our schools as it relates to our leadership. When principals leave the system, this negatively impacts student achievement because of the instability (Mahfouz et al., 2019). Also, many principal preparation programs do not teach social emotional competencies as being vital for those in leadership roles. Therefore, it may be challenging for principals to regulate the complex emotions and effectively handle the stress they will encounter as school leaders (Mahfouz et al., 2019).

Principals have a lot to balance when running their schools, and if they are not convinced of the need for change, it may not take a priority in their

Principal	Students	Dean/AP	Teachers	Student Services	Parents & Families	Educational Assistants	Community
Evaluation of SEL coach	Learning about their needs	SEL team meetings	Learning about their needs	Learning about their needs	Learning about their needs	Learning about their needs	Learning about SEL understanding
Promotion of SEL work at school	Tier 1 SEL instruction	Understanding discipline procedures	Coaching and PD	SEL team meetings	Workshops	Professional development	Connection to school
SEL team meetings	Observations & discussions	Problem-solving process	Adult SEL	Tier 2 & 3 SEL	Websites and newsletters	Adult SEL	Websites and newsletters

building. When discussing the urgency for change with principals, emphasize the positive outcomes that can occur after implementation. One must address any concerns or questions to get to the heart of any misconceptions.

The coach and administrator share the goal of effecting positive change. The administrator takes the lead in crafting a vision and presenting it to staff, but they are both charged with the monumental and complicated task of making that vision a reality. Three driving forces should always guide the behaviors of the administrators and the coach. They are building individual relationships with their educational stakeholders, increasing teacher capacity, and strengthening teams (Hall & Simeral, 2008). These driving forces are critical for SEL implementation as well. And principals are perfectly positioned to help create the environment where it can happen. The SEL coach should consider the following about their building principal or administrator.

REFLECTIONS

1. What does your administration/principal currently understand about Social Emotional Learning?

2. What is their level of buy-in? Specifically ask about time for meetings or professional development, resources, and the budget available.

3. Have they made regular, public statements of support? If not, are they willing to?

4. Are they actively working toward getting faculty and staff buy-in?

5. Are they willing to participate in SEL team meetings?

6. Will they work toward building a vision that supports this work?

7. Will they embed the vision in the decision-making process?

8. Will they reinforce actions that fall in line with the vision?

THE SEL COACH IS THE NAVIGATOR

As a navigator, being an effective communicator is key to your success. Prepare yourself for process changes by assessing the areas where you have influence. While your school community may find change challenging at first, remember that you are the navigator of the ship and can help your school move toward supporting students via proven SEL practices and processes. You will need to navigate the needs of your program and best practices with the principal, thus understanding the principal's perception and need for the SEL coaching role in the system.

It is critical to get your leadership on board before you can get this intervention off the ground. Principals play a critical role in the selection, effective implementation, and sustainability of SEL programs, policies, and practices (Mahfouz et al., 2019). Principal support is a key element, but not the only consideration that SEL coaches must consider. They are one part of the overall system. In future chapters, we will be looking at the important relationship between SEL coaches and other key educational stakeholders.

LESLIE LEDERMAN

Professional Development Director
and Former Building Principal

Washington

Interview:

1. *What did you find was most effective about the program or practice?*

   SEL implementation was needed and the tools we were provided initially were varied. Having a choice in the order of implementation gave us the flexibility to weave the demands of this initiative into our already full plates.

2. *What is the best way to increase schoolwide implementation of Social Emotional Learning in your experience?*

   Having a small group of leaders create a plan that includes the most impactful components of an SEL approach is the best first step. From there, each building can take that plan and complete a self-assessment to determine to which degree of success they had integrated each component. Using the self-assessment, they would then plan next steps.

3. *What was your specific role and contributions in the SEL implementation process?*

   I led the efforts at my building as the building principal.

4. *What was the first thing you did?*

   The first thing I had to do was to sell the idea to my staff. Next, we created a committee to manage the process, and finally, we began implementing pieces at our building.

5. *Were there any surprises?*

   Everything always takes more time than you think, and funding is never really enough or placed in the most effective way.

6. *What were the issues that you saw from a district perspective?*

   Unfortunately, the district leadership was not all on the same page, and this led to changes in staffing both at the district and building levels, which impacted the support and smooth implementation. As a result, the program became watered down and the focus shifted from this initiative to another. When launching the intervention is not thought through, the needs of the audience and the needs of the initiative are not met.

7. *What were the key sources of support or resistance you encountered?*

   "It's one more thing" is a mantra heard often in education. It is true and the district should have waited until they had full funding (time, materials, etc.). They jumped in without a complete plan and this caused staff to resist the change.

8. *What do you recommend for SEL coaches to get to know and serve administrators in a meaningful way? Are there things they could be doing to build that relationship quicker and stronger in your opinion?*

   Coaches should consult with principals and ask them, "What does your year look like?" prior to coming on board as the coach. They should let the staff know what their qualifications are and how those connect to supporting teachers. For example, share how the role you are leaving relates to their daily, classroom needs and explain how you plan to partner with them. As a principal, I am prepping my own professional development. If you accept the position, you have to understand that there should be time to meet with your building principal in the month leading up to the start of the school year. It is important to spend time watching how the world of your assigned school comes together to get some perspective. Develop relationships with everybody in the office and have those conversations around how a coach can get to know the teachers. A coach should expect to spend time developing relationships with all. For the first month, plan to spend time going to actively engage, not just passively observe, at the start of the day, in the lunchroom, in the hallways, during recess, and at the end of the day. Greet the kids and talk with them so they know who you are. In October, meet with each grade-level team and figure out how you can come into their classrooms to be in the background.

Better yet, find something you can do for the teachers you support in the classroom to create a presence and show the students that you belong here. You could offer to do something simple like going in to read a story. Look for low-level kinds of things that do not add to a teacher's plate but give you a chance to establish relationships with students and to show that you are there to support them. Continue having classroom visits and relationship building all year. In a nonevaluative way, let your principal know when and where you are seeing great things. After many months, possibly 5–6, offer to a teacher the opportunity to partner on a lesson.

As a coach, set aside time to have honest conversations with your principal. Discuss what is exciting to you, and what is worrying you, and ask for more help or clarification when needed. Let your principal know if a staff member is resistant and listen to advice on how best to approach that person. Letting teachers know that you are not coming to fix them, but rather that it is an honor to join them, is important.

9. *What is the best way to get feedback about the coach's work?*

As the coach works with staff, ask for feedback. Share that this is new and that you are interested in where the staff feels improvements can be made. Be transparent. If you know that a decision falls entirely on your shoulders as the principal, tell the staff. You can still share your thinking and invite guidance but state upfront that you have to ultimately be the decision maker. With all decisions that allow for their input, let your staff present their ideas or suggestions for improvement first. Listen to everyone and then present your position. Follow up with an invitation to "poke holes" in your thinking and then work to find consensus.

10. *What are the lessons you would pass on to other people in your role?*

Have patience, build your beliefs first, and then bring in the tangible changes to practice.

CHAPTER 3

....

GETTING SYSTEM READY FOR SOCIAL EMOTIONAL LEARNING

There are two common challenges in SEL implementation. The first is a wide definition in how educators define SEL and the second is the lack of consistent implementation (Allbright et al., 2019). To help educators have a more consistent understanding of SEL, the SEL coach should establish foundational learning of Social Emotional Learning. And to help with consistent implementation, the system should agree on a framework, plan for sustainability, focus on equity, a needs assessment to understand what is necessary, and an action plan. In this chapter, resources for each of these sections will be detailed.

FOUNDATIONAL LEARNING OF SOCIAL EMOTIONAL LEARNING

To prepare your educational stakeholders for SEL implementation, we must begin with enhancing their foundational learning. The introduction should cover the understandings that we currently have about what SEL is and is not and also the research to date and some of the exciting outcomes. We are seeing the influence of the need for SEL now more than ever. It is important that we become very clear about the definitions and impact of SEL and use this momentum to forward our efforts in helping students and adults obtain these crucial social emotional competencies.

General Understandings About SEL

- Most research has been concentrated around five specific competencies (Jagers et al., 2018):

- Self-awareness has been defined as understanding one's emotions, personal identity, goals, and values. This includes accurately assessing one's strengths and limitations, having a positive mindset, possessing a well-grounded sense of self-efficacy, and optimism. High levels of self-awareness require the ability to understand the links between one's personal and sociocultural identities and to recognize how thoughts, feelings, and actions are interconnected.

- Self-management has been defined as the skills and attitudes that facilitate the ability to regulate emotions and behaviors. This includes the ability to delay gratification, manage stress, control impulses, and persevere through personal and group-level challenges to achieve personal and educational goals.

- Social awareness has been defined as the ability to take the perspective of those with the same and different backgrounds and cultures and to empathize and feel compassion. It also involves understanding social norms for behavior in diverse settings and recognizing family, school, and community resources and supports.

- Relationship skill has been defined as having the tools needed to establish and maintain healthy and rewarding relationships, and to effectively navigate settings with differing social norms and demands. It involves communicating clearly, listening actively, cooperating, resisting inappropriate social pressure, negotiating conflict constructively, and seeking help when it is needed.

- Responsible decision-making has been defined as having the knowledge, skills, and attitudes to make caring, constructive choices about personal behavior and social interactions across diverse settings. It requires the ability to critically examine ethical standards, safety concerns, and behavioral norms for risky behavior; to make realistic evaluations of consequences of various interpersonal and institutional actions; and to take the health and well-being of self and others into consideration.

- Social Emotional Learning IS (Jones et al., 2019):
  - Concrete, specific, observable, teachable skills
  - Evidence based (a large number of individual studies) that reveal the promise and impact of SEL
  - Focus on domains of social and emotional competencies (appropriate for educational environments)
  - Developmentally based

- Social Emotional Learning IS NOT (Jones et al., 2019):
  - Focused on personality constructs (conscientiousness)
  - Focused on broad dispositions (attitude)
  - Focused on traits (introversion)
  - Synonym for mental health (social and emotional competencies are just one piece of the larger scope of mental health)

- The impacts of SEL are long lasting. School-based, universal SEL interventions led to significant improvement in skills, dispositions, prosocial behavior, and academic performance at follow-up periods ranging from 56 to 195 weeks (Taylor et al., 2017).

- Research-based outcomes of Social Emotional Learning implementation include (Durlak et al., 2011):
  - Short-term outcomes: Social and emotional competencies and positive attitudes toward self, others, and school
  - Long-term outcomes: positive social behavior, decreased conduct problems, decreased emotional distress, increased engagement, and improved academic performance

- Benefits for teachers using SEL include:
  - In classrooms in which SEL is implemented effectively, teachers need to spend less time on classroom management (Jennings & Greenberg, 2009)
  - Feeling competent in implementing SEL in the classroom has been linked to experiencing a less disruptive and more positive classroom climate (Collie et al., 2012)
  - When teachers resort to reactive and punitive approaches, teachers often feel emotional exhaustion and find themselves in a burnout cascade (Marzano et al., 2003)

- SEL is effective and sustained if it:
  - Integrates SEL across grade levels
  - Takes a whole school approach that infuses SEL into practices and policies
  - Provides ongoing training and consultation
  - Engages families and community partners in program selection, refinement, and improvement and reinforces skill development at home (Brackett et al., 2019)

What are some other pieces of foundational learning for Social Emotional Learning that your stakeholders can use to enhance their understanding?

_____

_____

_____

_____

These are the distilled research findings that support our work as SEL implementers. It is important for the educational stakeholders to understand these foundational elements to promote Social Emotional Learning that is effective and sustained. With the current emphasis and excitement around SEL, it can become something that it is not. Thus, it is important to recognize that Social Emotional Learning and mental health are not the same things. Social and emotional competencies enhance mental health. They are protective factors that help students and adults navigate the complex world around us. Mental health is a huge construct that involves many things that are not necessarily appropriate for educators to work on in a school setting. But educators are perfectly capable of helping students learn to practice things such as empathy, problem-solving, emotional regulation, making friends, establishing boundaries, and having difficult conversations. These are skills that help students succeed academically and in life outside of school. We need to concentrate our efforts on teachable skills that help students and adults manage their relationships and emotions appropriately and become resilient.

SYSTEMIC IMPLEMENTATION OF SEL

SEL coaches help to introduce, manage, and lead the education of SEL for educational stakeholders and the school community. These roles provide the invaluable link between what we know and how we do it. The goal of the SEL coach is to support the school or district in effectively implementing SEL that makes sense for the unique strengths and challenges they face. Every school is different. Therefore, the approach to SEL implementation should take this into account. The first thing that the SEL coach will need to understand is their own people. Once you can understand your people, their needs, their beliefs and the barriers, and the infrastructure that will be needed to support your implementation, you will have the best chance at success. Social emotional competencies affect everyone in the system. Your coach role will be to guide your educational stakeholders through the ups and downs of implementation. Learning about your students, staff, parents/families, and community will help you to create action plans that will move the work forward in meaningful ways.

Investing in a Framework

Once the stakeholders understand more about SEL and there is buy-in for adopting practices and processes that will accelerate implementation, a framework should be chosen. A framework is an organized structure used to view concepts and practices. It is often seen as the *how-to* support for conducting the implementation efforts. Adopting a framework is an important next step after identifying your *why* for SEL. A framework provides us with a structure to guide our efforts. SEL coaches will benefit from having a logical order to follow. The framework I support is the one in the book *Leading for Change: Advocating for Positive School Culture Through Whole School Social Emotional Learning.*

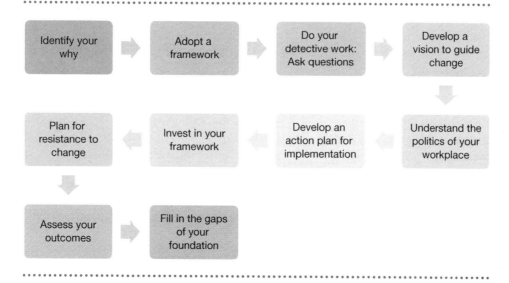

We need to do more to support school personnel to create school environments that are positive and productive. We need to provide them with the tools and strategies that will help them make their vision into reality—strategies that can be adopted by individuals and groups, teachers, administrators, counselors, and all other school personnel. Educators need the tools to engage in a process that is unique to their school or district but is rooted in evidence and experience. This framework is designed to help educators meet the challenges of implementation of Social Emotional Learning in their environments (Rogers, 2019). CASEL (Collaboration for Academic, Social Emotional Learning) also offers a systemic framework to look at SEL implementation. But it will be helpful to include a framework specifically for the work of SEL coaches.

FRAMEWORK FOR SEL COACHES: PRACTICE AND PROCESS

An SEL coach must consider both practice and process. The interventions, models, frameworks, and curriculums that are evidence or research based keep our implementation grounded in best practices. But the practices don't always make room for the unique qualities of your school or district. That is why an SEL coach must also focus on process—the way in which the individuals in a system manage change and new ways of thinking and working. The metaphor I like to use is that your practice is the boat, the process is the river that you are trying to get down to reach your destination. When deciding on what practices you need to successfully make the journey, you must also consider the unpredictability of the water (the process). Some days it will be smooth sailing and other days you will feel like you are about to capsize. As mentioned previously, the SEL coach's role is the navigator. And the administration is the captain. You are there to advise them and design the best route and also problem solve when an unexpected storm arises. It can be very difficult to navigate when the coach has one vision, and the administration and staff have another vision. Communication is vital for establishing a united vision between what you know about the benefits and outcomes of SEL and the vision that considers what the principal wants for their school. It is important to understand what the principal's vision is for the school. And when that principal leaves, you will also need to understand what the next principal's vision for the school is.

This graphic shows how the system and the SEL coach work together to create an action plan for systemic SEL.

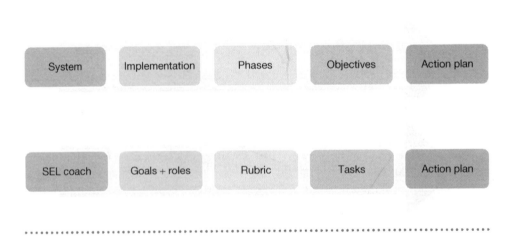

BEGINNING WITH THE END IN MIND: THE ISSUE OF SUSTAINABILITY

Sustainability is the overall goal of your SEL implementation efforts. Investing in practices that will continue year over year no matter who is the principal or SEL coach. Researchers have determined that the sustainability features of administrative support combined with communication and data-based decision-making create the best-fitting model of sustainability for educational innovations (Coffey & Horner, 2012). Sustained practice of evidence-based practices is currently one of the more complex things for us to reliably replicate. This is especially true with the current nature of administrators moving from school to school or district to district. As of 2016–2017, the national average tenure of principals in their schools was four years (Levin & Bradley, 2019). These numbers vary with 35 percent of principals being at their school for less than two years and only 11 percent of principals being at their school for 10 years or more (Levin & Bradley, 2019). This is a conundrum for many SEL coaches. How are we to make things sustainable when one of the major components of sustainability moves on an average of every four years? The answer is to embed the practices in teachers instead. Teachers are much more likely to stay in a school where they feel comfortable and supported. When administrators move, it can often be out of their control and may instead be a district's decision. The SEL coach can embed sustainable practices by making SEL live through the educational stakeholders.

According to Centola (2021), adoption of an innovation requires the following:

1. Coordination: Some innovations are appealing only if people use them together; they require social reinforcement to spread. The more people who adopt, the more valuable the innovation becomes and the easier to spread.

2. Credibility: Skepticism about effectiveness; the more they adopt, the less risky it seems; repeated confirmation by trusted others overcomes the credibility barrier.

3. Legitimacy: Social approval to reduce embarrassment or tarnished reputation; social reinforcement from respected peers overcomes the legitimacy barrier.

4. Excitement: Some innovations are appealing only when people are emotionally energized by one another; social reinforcement among energized peers is essential for these emotional contagions to spread (Centola, 2021).

The tipping point of any change is for 25% of dedicated users of SEL to shift. But the real challenge lies in not developing solutions but convincing those people to use them regularly (Centola, 2021).

FOCUS ON EQUITY

Equity of service is critical for all students. It will be important for the SEL coach to consider how to achieve equity in their school. What actionable steps make the most sense? The recommendations, according to a 2018 report by Penn State and Robert Wood Johnson Foundation (Simmons et al., 2018), focus on the five barriers contributing to inequitable access: poverty, implicit bias in school staff, exclusionary discipline practices and policies, lack of trauma-informed school practices, and educators' stress and burnout.

SELF-REFLECTION

What is your school leadership/SEL team doing to focus on equity?

Focus on students/families who are in poverty: What social and emotional resources are devoted to children in poverty?

_____

_____

_____

_____

Focus on trauma-informed school practices: What are your current trauma-informed practices? How are they braided with SEL?

_____

_____

_____

_____

Focus on educator stress and burnout: What resources are devoted to helping teachers learn more about self-compassion and self-care? How are educators encouraged to practice self-care?

_____

_____

_____

_____

Focus on implicit bias in school staff: How do we understand the conditions under which we become more vulnerable to implicit bias? When we're thinking fast and moving fast, we are more likely to make biased decisions. How can we promote educators to slow down and make a shift so we're less likely to act on our biases?

_____

_____

_____

_____

Focus on exclusionary discipline practices and policies: What do your current discipline practices look like? Is there disproportionality in the students who receive exclusionary consequences?

_____

_____

_____

_____

One of the best practices for maximizing the success of interventions is to be sensitive to cultural diversity in the consultation and intervention process (Rathvon, 2008). SEL coaches need to be aware of their own cultural values and the biases of others involved in the process of implementation. It is especially important to understand how the perceptions, even subconsciously, of students' racial, ethnic, or linguistic backgrounds can influence the decision process. The SEL coach will need to examine the impact of cultural and linguistic differences of the students and staff in the problem-solving process, the level of acceptance for specific interventions, and teaming strategies (Rathvon, 2008).

In your work, this is an area worth more investigation. The SEL coach may be involved in collecting data around equity practices. Once you have those understandings, recommendations can be made to focus efforts toward greater equity and create opportunities for discussion and learning around cultural bias, parental support, student behavior, motivation, and punitive discipline. It is imperative to understand what is behind these statements. Self-awareness can be enhanced when we examine social identities and affirm cultural heritage. And social awareness can be enhanced when we understand situational and contextual diversity and build collective efficacy (Jagers et al., 2018).

CONDUCT A NEEDS ASSESSMENT

To effectively meet the needs of your school community, you'll need to determine what those needs are. One of the first tasks on your action plan will be to conduct a needs assessment. The purpose of a needs assessment is to identify areas of opportunity within your system using data provided by your school and from interviews you conduct with teachers, students, and administrators.

Understand your specific school/s. Understand the data, demographics, and how school is perceived.

- Does your school have a strong parent network?

- Is there cultural diversity? What does that look like?

- What are the extracurricular activities that take place?

- What commentary is being written in sites like Great Schools?

- What is the free/reduced lunch rate?

- What is the population of students who qualify for SE services?

- What are the academic expectations at the school?

- What is the school climate like?

- What is the student/teacher ratio?

- How are the students who are English language learners (ELL) served?

Are your schools using a specific SEL or Positive Behavior or another schoolwide programming that focuses on behavior? What are the perceptions of the students of the program? The teachers? The administration? All other stakeholders? Systematically review to identify strengths and gaps in current programming. Have any teachers integrated social emotional programming into their academic instruction? What are the qualities of the instruction that are impactful to the students?

Conducting a needs assessment will help you understand the data, demographics, and how your school is perceived. Systematically review these factors and data points to identify strengths and gaps in current programming. This is vital before starting any change initiative. You may never have all the information. But endeavoring to be as clear about your current system is beneficial. It is difficult to know where to go if you don't know where you are.

AN ACTION PLAN FOR SYSTEMWIDE CLARITY

Action plans will play an important role in implementing SEL interventions in your system. A strong action plan provides a road map for you to follow and will ensure that you maintain effective and clear communication with others in your school. Action plans, especially when created collaboratively and shared with others, will help your school change and readily accept it. Action plans should be carefully planned and implemented. Is there a specific structure or timeline that is guiding the implementation? What are the district expectations for schools and timeline?

Phased Implementation Model

Leaders will likely focus on timelines. Most of their work is built that way. So, if we tell them that implementation is indefinite or as long as it takes, we may not get the buy-in that we need. Each school is in a unique place. From staff readiness to commitment to implementation of next phases to experience with elements of SEL, each school is on its own journey that will be hard to capture in phases that are bound by specific timelines. You will also need to think about district and school needs. Collaborate with school leadership to create a document that describes process objectives and the phases of work that depict the central items to practice SEL implementation. These two should be coordinated in the sense that schools will know when resources would be available for schools ready to effectively use them. It is recommended that schools, with full staff participation, create building action plans for the next year(s) of SEL implementation. This would provide clarity and an opportunity for feedback. This could also provide the district with a greater understanding of the resources needed and any identified barriers to implementation. That is why creating a phased action plan can be beneficial. Individual schools can be working on a phase for as long as they need to move the work forward. Because it seems that some buildings may need years on one aspect of SEL, such as universal implementation or Tier 2 Interventions, to make meaningful progress. Individual schools should create a road map or plan for implementation across a few years. And they can use a school screener to determine the baseline for school. Meanwhile, SEL coaches will begin by understanding and getting to know your staff at your school and gathering data about programs currently in use and their effectiveness. Coaches will begin developing a team to deliver feedback and talk about the data, and they will also begin to provide professional development to the school through whole school meetings, teacher groups, EA groups, and individual teachers to enhance foundational learnings.

This is important to create as soon as possible for everyone to have a clear idea of the direction they are going in. The document that lists the action steps, each phase, the subsections, and who is responsible for each practice can be very complex.

This rubric has been designed to examine how systemic implementation and the roles of the SEL coach work together. The first column shows the areas of systemic implementation for SEL. These are things that leadership and the SEL coach will want to look to as the framework that guides the work. The second column is the key roles and responsibilities of the SEL coach. Next are the process objectives—things that may not be put on a checklist but guide your "way of being." The phases are the steps to help SEL implementation come to life. These are actionable things that can be done to teach, practice, model, and support SEL. The purpose of using this instrument or something like it is to give SEL implementers a tool to measure the efforts.

SYSTEMIC IMPLEMENTATION	SEL COACH RESPONSIBILITY	PROCESS OBJECTIVES	PHASE 1: UNDERSTAND WHAT IS CURRENTLY HAPPENING IN YOUR SYSTEM	PHASE 2: CHOOSE STRATEGIES TO MEET THE NEEDS OF THE STUDENTS AND EDUCATORS	PHASE 3: EVALUATE ALL SCHOOLWIDE CHOSEN STRATEGIES	PHASE 4: DETERMINE WHICH PRACTICES BECOME PART OF SCHOOL CULTURE
Vision and goals	Leader or facilitator	• Support vision through collaboration with stakeholders • Develop goals in collaboration with stakeholders • Influence school culture in a positive way • Commit to equity • Build relationships with stakeholders, teachers, and staff • Promote understanding of SEL • Positively report and promote the progress being made by students, staff, and the community as it relates to your endeavors	• Learn about your school or district's vision and goals • Have discussions with administration about expectations of new SEL role • Determine your relationships with staff • Conduct a belief survey • Inventory stakeholders' knowledge of SEL • Inventory programs and initiatives • Consider organizational capacity for practices and processes	• Make success visible • Create narratives to make prevention live • Create a process to determine which strategy, program, and intervention to try • Determine strategies to promote student engagement	• Braid your initiatives • Create a process for targeted (Tier 2) interventions • Enhance student voice by creating a youth advisory board • Develop an intervention matrix	• Create a year-at-a-glance document • Create an SEL universal prevention manual for chosen practices • Collect and organize resources

SYSTEMIC IMPLEMENTATION	SEL COACH RESPONSIBILITY	PROCESS OBJECTIVES	PHASE 1: UNDERSTAND WHAT IS CURRENTLY HAPPENING IN YOUR SYSTEM	PHASE 2: CHOOSE STRATEGIES TO MEET THE NEEDS OF THE STUDENTS AND EDUCATORS	PHASE 3: EVALUATE ALL SCHOOLWIDE CHOSEN STRATEGIES	PHASE 4: DETERMINE WHICH PRACTICES BECOME PART OF SCHOOL CULTURE
System readiness	Coach	• Work directly with staff to implement interventions and teach the selected program • Understand and promote prevention (Tier 1) work as the foundation • Use different modalities to coach staff based on their needs • Discover procedure to access individuals who may need help • Acknowledge positive practices of staff and students and celebrate accomplishments	• Get clarity for the SEL coach role for staff • Interview administration on SEL coach • Introduce SEL coach role to staff • Educate stakeholders about the SEL coach role • Determine precedence for observations • Assess adult SEL practices	• Create a form for SEL coaching support • Connecting social and emotional competencies with individual skills • Practice collaborative conversations • Share the positives of your SEL implementation	• Build collaborative relationships through staff empowerment • Create and use an observation template • Develop a sense of ownership in SEL implementation • Build adult SEL teacher capacity	• Reflect on confidentiality and expectations of the SEL coaching role • Plan for working through resistance • Develop a support request form • Monitor the effectiveness of the SEL coaching role

(Continued)

(Continued)

SYSTEMIC IMPLEMENTATION	SEL COACH RESPONSIBILITY	PROCESS OBJECTIVES	PHASE 1: UNDERSTAND WHAT IS CURRENTLY HAPPENING IN YOUR SYSTEM	PHASE 2: CHOOSE STRATEGIES TO MEET THE NEEDS OF THE STUDENTS AND EDUCATORS	PHASE 3: EVALUATE ALL SCHOOLWIDE CHOSEN STRATEGIES	PHASE 4: DETERMINE WHICH PRACTICES BECOME PART OF SCHOOL CULTURE
Measuring outcomes	Data collection and analysis	• Identify and collect current data • Identify gaps and encourage new ways of gaining missing data • Focus on data to support student outcomes • Monitor progress to aid in the decision-making process • Help in the implementation of screening and assessment measures • Develop plans for results of data • Conduct periodic surveys of staff and students to gauge effectiveness	• Get training in qualitative and quantitative methods of data collection and analysis • Understand historical data with school snapshot • Use culture or climate assessments to create a social and emotional competence data set	• Create SMART goals • Process for in-the-moment data collection • Create a resource map for universal screener data	• Create or adopt a problem-solving process • Create or adopt a tiered fidelity inventory	• Learn more about strategies used by individual teachers • Develop an evaluation document

SYSTEMIC IMPLEMENTATION	SEL COACH RESPONSIBILITY	PROCESS OBJECTIVES	PHASE 1: UNDERSTAND WHAT IS CURRENTLY HAPPENING IN YOUR SYSTEM	PHASE 2: CHOOSE STRATEGIES TO MEET THE NEEDS OF THE STUDENTS AND EDUCATORS	PHASE 3: EVALUATE ALL SCHOOLWIDE CHOSEN STRATEGIES	PHASE 4: DETERMINE WHICH PRACTICES BECOME PART OF SCHOOL CULTURE
SEL Teams	Team leader	• Establish commitment of team members at school • Facilitate a data-based decision-making process • Create an environment that is both supportive and focused on achieving goals	• Determine the best people for the SEL team and invite them to participate • Assign team roles • Create general shared commitments • Create meeting forms (agenda, action plan, etc.) • Choose norms in collaboration with the team • Determine how SEL teams work with other school teams • Adopt an SEL team meeting minutes document • Introduce the SEL team to staff	• Agree on consensus practices • Create a feedback process for the communication strategies with team input • Plan ways to motivate your team • Determine how the team is functioning • Recruit and train new members of the team (year over year)	• Work on data analysis with the SEL team • Attune to your SEL team	• Check in with selected educational stakeholders

(Continued)

(Continued)

SYSTEMIC IMPLEMENTATION	SEL COACH RESPONSIBILITY	PROCESS OBJECTIVES	PHASE 1: UNDERSTAND WHAT IS CURRENTLY HAPPENING IN YOUR SYSTEM	PHASE 2: CHOOSE STRATEGIES TO MEET THE NEEDS OF THE STUDENTS AND EDUCATORS	PHASE 3: EVALUATE ALL SCHOOLWIDE CHOSEN STRATEGIES	PHASE 4: DETERMINE WHICH PRACTICES BECOME PART OF SCHOOL CULTURE
Schoolwide practices	Professional development	• Create awareness and understanding of concepts • Use multiple modalities to engage the audience • Inform staff of evidence-based practices • Engage staff in learning and empowering their voice in the process	• Answer introductory questions about universal SEL through PD • Build educator capacity • Prepare for professional development • Investigate the current and proposed SEL interventions • Deliver professional development	• Choose interventions and make educational stakeholders understand why they were chosen • Scaffold trainings for interventions • Enhance classroom procedures after PD	• Engage in the self-reflection process • Learn from others' experiences through exit tickets • Determine the efficacy of professional development	• Maximize outside trainings • Create a scope and sequence document • Build an action plan for schoolwide practices by role
Yearly reporting	Communication	• Share practices used by different stakeholders throughout the system	• Create a communication flowchart to gauge areas of need	• Engage parents and families in the work	• Communicate about problem areas	• Invest in community stakeholders

(Continued)

SYSTEMIC IMPLEMENTATION	SEL COACH RESPONSIBILITY	PROCESS OBJECTIVES	PHASE 1: UNDERSTAND WHAT IS CURRENTLY HAPPENING IN YOUR SYSTEM	PHASE 2: CHOOSE STRATEGIES TO MEET THE NEEDS OF THE STUDENTS AND EDUCATORS	PHASE 3: EVALUATE ALL SCHOOLWIDE CHOSEN STRATEGIES	PHASE 4: DETERMINE WHICH PRACTICES BECOME PART OF SCHOOL CULTURE
		• Possess the ability to listen actively, summarize, and make actionable the things that are needed by the stakeholders • Work in collaborative relationships with different individuals and teams • Advocate for the needs of the program and process • Model effective interpersonal communication skills	• Brainstorm with collaboration partners • Determine ways to communicate with stakeholders • Create a pitch for the work of the SEL coach • Create a yearly report	• Create a parent/family education team • Develop parent/family workshops • Collect data from parents/families • Create a yearly report	• Communicate recommendations • Get testimonials from teachers • Create a yearly report	• Let your community know about your good work • Create a yearly report
			Total tasks completed=	Total tasks completed=	Total tasks completed=	Total tasks completed=

CHAPTER 4

....

ADVANCE YOUR PRACTICE

Leader/Facilitator

In the leader or facilitator role, the SEL coach will be supporting the following objectives: support vision through collaboration with stakeholders; develop goals in collaboration with stakeholders; influence school culture in a positive way; commit to equity; build relationships with students, stakeholders, teachers, and staff; promote understanding of SEL; and promote the progress being made by students, staff, and community as it relates to your endeavors. The purpose is to build a foundation required to support implementation.

As a leader, you will be responsible for understanding your staff's SEL implementation needs and developing the processes and procedures to meet their needs. Creating these procedures will require leadership skills in organizing and promoting the work so it will be used by the educational stakeholders. Things like the intervention matrix can be helpful for all educational stakeholders so the team does not keep having to reinvent the wheel. The SEL coach will have to lead, organize, and create with others to develop such resources.

The SEL coach will need to think about the effects on the system and how the practices and processes braid together. It may be helpful to consider the phases of the rollout and the tasks that go along with it. The work is broken up into phases. They are not based on specific timelines but rather on a logical progression of skill sets.

PHASE 1: LEADERSHIP AND FACILITATOR ROLE TASKS

Learning About the District Vision Statement

A vision statement is a one-sentence statement that describes the change resulting in the implementation of the program/process. A mission statement describes the why or reason for the change and it is used to create goals and priorities. A feedback loop should be considered that addresses how information routes through the system: state, superintendent, principal, leadership team, staff via professional development back to team with feedback at staff. Begin with the vision statement and have as many stakeholders offer feedback in the creation of the vision (Rogers, 2019).

When collaborating with educational stakeholders, the why should drive the need and must be included in the rationale/vision. This is the best way to influence teachers. Many teachers can agree with the concepts of student-centered learning environments and focus on relationship, social and emotional growth, and real-world learning. But do they make it central to every decision they make? Another important component when fleshing out the vision and goals of system change is to connect to school realities. Will this help them with their day-to-day responsibilities, their evaluation system, and how it connects to the realities of teaching?

Investing others in schoolwide SEL goals and an SEL vision can be challenging. Change can be difficult for some, and you'll need to meet each person where they are. Remember that your role includes being a change agent and implementing strategies to encourage others to buy in to any changes you're proposing. To craft your vision, you may need to make it live first. Discuss with your stakeholders the findings. Use data, examples, stories, research, scenarios, and any other strategies to showcase the positive benefits of SEL schoolwide. You may be wondering, "How can I invest others in the idea that the changes I'm proposing are right for our school?" You're not alone. Investing others in your school in the idea that SEL needs are vital may not always be easy, but it is possible.

TASK: Reflect on current school/district vision

What is your school's vision and mission? Your district?

_____

_____

_____

_____

How can it be connected to your SEL efforts?

_____

_____

_____

_____

School Readiness: Working With Administrators

Speaking with the principal at your school is important when creating an action plan. While there are many ways to gather information, the principal will have the most information about their school, students, and gaps in SEL. Focus on team structure, staff introductions, and working collaboratively during your conversation. When you meet with your school leader, you will need to ask questions about their plans for teams, structures, and SEL vision. This is your opportunity to discover how to be an effective navigator.

First, the SEL coach should learn more about the understanding of the principal's perception/need for the coaching role. The SEL coach's role is to navigate the needs of the program and best practices with the principal. Coaches will need to prepare for conversations about boundaries. This includes playing "all hands on deck" while establishing boundaries—for example, subbing for teachers on a regular basis. Consider what your plan is when the principal is asking you to do things that are not the coaches' responsibilities. Determine whether this the right time, place, and person to talk to about this?

For some principals, there will be little understanding of SEL and there may be a need to coach the administrators. You may want to ask a few questions to deal with difficult conversations (Kofman, 2014). They include the following:

1. "What do you think?" (General interpretation)

2. "What leads you to think what you think?" (Facts and reasoning)

3. "What would you like to accomplish?" (Goal)

4. "What is the most important thing to you?" (Concern)

5. "What do you suggest we do?" (Proposal for concrete actions)

The discussions with principals should include the best plan for implementation rollout. This could be a pilot or whole school. You navigate your role keeping in mind not only the system but also the principal's needs. You may want to prepare to discuss the following:

Task: Discuss the expectations of the SEL role with administrators

- How do we monitor the efficacy of the classroom/teacher support/coaching conversations and approaches?

- How do we promote effective leadership skills to coordinate with each other?

- What should data look like and what function does it have? What level of consistency is expected?

Positive School Culture Through Positive Relationships

If your school's environment is warm, inviting, and positive, both teachers and students will benefit. Students who feel connected to their schools and have positive relationships with their teachers are more likely to be successful (Hamre & Pianta, 2006). Teachers thrive in a culture that values their contributions and promotes trust and collaboration. As an SEL leader, you'll always be asking the question "How can we ensure our culture is positive for both students and adults?" and taking action to make your school's culture a safe and more positive place for everyone.

One critical aspect of forming a positive school culture is the development of strong, positive relationships between students and teachers. Student outcomes can be directly connected to the quality of their relationships with their teachers. When a student has a negative relationship with a teacher, their achievement is impacted. And when a student feels positive toward and connected with their teacher, they are more likely to succeed (Hamre & Pianta, 2006).

As the SEL leader, your role will be to empower both students and teachers to cultivate strong social and emotional competencies. This will enhance their relationships and positively impact student performance outcomes and overall well-being. But as with all things, practices begin with the SEL coach. How can the SEL coach reflect on their own relationships in the school building?

Relationship Reflection

How does your staff know that you believe in them?

_____

_____

_____

_____

Which staff members do you know well and have a trusting relationship with?

_____

_____

_____

_____

Which staff members do you need to get to know better—or restore a relationship with if something happened to disrupt your trust?

_____

_____

_____

_____

What strategy will you try to build intentional relationships with your staff?

_____

_____

_____

_____

Understanding Beliefs

There are many different types of belief surveys that can be useful in understanding your educational stakeholders. To successfully implement evidence-based practices within your school, it is important to assess and understand the overall beliefs of the staff. Educators' beliefs and attitudes are a major component of any systemic change in practices and improvement in outcomes within schools (Gusky, 1988). Teachers' beliefs can affect both implementation fidelity and willingness to adopt social emotional learning curricula (Reyes et al., 2012). Teachers are instrumental in the execution and impact of SEL. Central to effective SEL program adoption and continuation are the attitudes and beliefs teachers have about SEL in general and their ability to implement the program and model the behavior to children (Elbertson et al., 2010).

The purpose of using a belief survey is to examine the relationship between beliefs, practices, and student outcomes. The SEL coach will want to understand educator beliefs through surveys or questionnaires. These instruments are created to measure beliefs about students' social emotional and behavioral functioning. Researchers have found that beliefs are critical to the implementation and fidelity of interventions (Cook et al., 2015).

TASK: Conduct a belief survey

To connect the dots and provide clarity for your educational stakeholders, you may want to consider using a graphic to describe what the belief is, how your staff scored, and what sort of intervention can be used to mediate this score.

Example:

BELIEF	DATA	INTERVENTION
Teaching social and emotional competencies is part of my responsibility as a teacher.	79% of staff agreed or strongly agreed.	Teach, model, and reinforce social and emotional skills.

As part of your action plan, you can use the results of belief surveys to continue work that the staff already agrees with. For example, if teachers believe in positive relationships with students, the strategy is to create an intentional practice by using positive greetings at the door. Or it can be used to examine beliefs that the staff has that don't promote acceptance of the interventions. For example, staff that scored low on the belief of extrinsic motivation can have discussions about what the research says about the role of extrinsic motivation and behavior, and they can move in a direction closer to trying a schoolwide motivation system.

Know What Your People Know About SEL

Before you can make any meaningful change, you will need to understand more about what your educational stakeholders know about the important components of your SEL implementation. It will be important to learn more about the educational environment. Initial meetings set the tone for your relationships and your school community. It also gives you the opportunity to meet with critical members of the community. During your meetings, make sure to convey your overall goals for the community and encourage collaboration with team members.

These meetings with administrators include getting direction from the district and administration that tells us where we all want to land in whatever amount of time. So, regardless of the path we take to get there, where do we need to be and at what time? You may also need to understand more about union commitments, if applicable to your work.

It is also important to recognize the impact of noncertified educators/paraprofessionals in your school community. SEL coaches are there to get to know not only certified staff but also the classified staff, including bus drivers, kitchen staff, and secretaries. Some ideas for furthering this communication are to provide recognition for speaking out and attending meetings. If they need to talk, make sure you can listen. Discuss what positive and intentional relationships mean to them and how they practice them. Recognize what they are doing and support them in learning new strategies. Make them feel that they are a part of the SEL implementation because they are an important part of the school culture.

It will be critical to move your people and coalesce around a common goal that has systemwide buy-in. That includes the flexibility for understanding that not all reasons are the same for wanting to implement SEL. And not everyone has the same understanding of what SEL is and what its purpose is. This lack of understanding can result in something called a silent conspiracy: where people do not actively engage in the implementation, even if they passively agree to do so.

SEL coaches must make the processes and practices that involve SEL implementation as transparent as possible. This will include open conversations about previous educational programming. It can help for staff to know that SEL is not just another passing fad. Educators need proof or reassurance that it is here to stay and know who's on board from a leadership level. The following SEL General Knowledge Inventory can help SEL coaches understand where each stakeholder group stands.

Task: Inventory SEL general knowledge

SEL General Knowledge Inventory

Take a moment and look at the statements in the left column. Consider the people you work with in your district and the parent/community population. Check all boxes that you believe stakeholders understand about Social Emotional Learning. Then for the ones that don't have a check, make a star in the box if you think it would be beneficial for them to know. NOTE: P/C = parent/community.

INVENTORY OF KNOWLEDGE

DO THEY KNOW ABOUT . . .	TEAM	DISTRICT	PRINCIPALS	TEACHERS	CLASSIFIED	STUDENTS	P/C	TOTAL
The 5 SEL Core Competencies	☐	☐	☐	☐	☐	☐	☐	
That SEL is proven to increase academic achievement	☐	☐	☐	☐	☐	☐	☐	
That SEL implementation has been found to improve dropout rates, school and classroom behavior issues, drug use, teen pregnancy, mental health issues, and criminal behavior	☐	☐	☐	☐	☐	☐	☐	
That SEL has a strong return on investment in that for every dollar invested there is an economic return of 11 dollars	☐	☐	☐	☐	☐	☐	☐	
There are four recommended SEL approaches: explicit instruction, daily teacher practices, integration with academics, and organizational strategies	☐	☐	☐	☐	☐	☐	☐	

INVENTORY OF KNOWLEDGE

DO THEY KNOW ABOUT . . .	TEAM	DISTRICT	PRINCIPALS	TEACHERS	CLASSIFIED	STUDENTS	P/C	TOTAL
Aware of the SAFE (sequenced, active, focused, explicit) component of effective SEL	☐	☐	☐	☐	☐	☐	☐	
Understand that SEL is for everyone	☐	☐	☐	☐	☐	☐	☐	
SEL is prevention and intervention	☐	☐	☐	☐	☐	☐	☐	
SEL is beneficial for students and adults	☐	☐	☐	☐	☐	☐	☐	
It is important to use data when determining the emphasis of your SEL implementation	☐	☐	☐	☐	☐	☐	☐	
Social and emotional competencies should be developmentally appropriate	☐	☐	☐	☐	☐	☐	☐	
SEL is more than a curriculum taught on a schedule	☐	☐	☐	☐	☐	☐	☐	

Inventory Programs and Initiatives

As you begin to understand more about what you are currently doing as a system, and whether it works or not, part of your role as leader/facilitator will be to create processes and procedures that are easy to follow. The inventory is one of those examples you may consider creating for your SEL implementation. This can be especially helpful for your educational stakeholders to go through.

TASK: Inventory programs and initiatives

PROGRAM	PURPOSE	TARGETED GROUP	EXPECTED OUTCOME	EVIDENCE OF FIDELITY	OUTCOME DATA (IS IT WORKING?)

Determining the specific needs for your SEL intervention may require an intervention matrix, an intervention manual, and a procedure for organizing your resources which will be demonstrated in later phases.

Organizational Capacity: Practices and Processes

The SEL coach must account for factors that affect the efficacy of SEL implementation. One of those things is organizational capacity. Some of the general organizational factors include the educational stakeholder's perception of a positive work climate which includes trust, collegiality, openness to change, risk-taking, willingness to try new things, shared vision, and staff buy-in (Durlak & DuPre, 2008). Along with that are the specific practices and processes that help to promote the use of SEL systemically. This includes shared decision-making, coordination across the system and with outside partnerships, and procedures to enhance the ability to strategically plan (Durlak & DuPre, 2008). The SEL coach is there to help champion the efforts of implementation by the teachers and staff. They can advocate for staff to give them the needed support for trying something new. As we know, new practice adoption can be difficult and scary.

How is trust demonstrated between colleagues at school?

_____

_____

_____

_____

How often do the teachers enjoy working together?

_____

_____

_____

_____

Think of an example of openness to change or risk-taking from your staff.

_____

_____

_____

_____

Is your staff generally willing to try new things? Do you have an example?

_____

_____

_____

_____

Does your staff share in the vision of SEL, and what is the level of buy-in?

_____

_____

_____

_____

PHASE 2: LEADERSHIP AND FACILITATOR ROLE TASKS

Focus on the Importance of Prevention

We can learn a lot from the medical field and its approach to prevention when considering our efforts at increasing social and emotional competencies. When we think of prevention, we are considering reducing the risk of poor outcomes. In an educational setting, this can mean things such as bullying, drop-out rate, violence, self-harm, drug use, and so on. If the students are involved in risky behaviors, it is likely that there is an impact on them both inside and outside of the school day.

The Centers for Disease Control and Prevention attempts to identify the health-risk behaviors that contribute to the leading causes of disease and death in youth throughout the country. They use the Youth Risk Behavior Surveillance System (YRBSS), which identifies six categories of priority health-related behaviors among youth and young adults: (1) behaviors that contribute to unintentional injuries and violence; (2) tobacco use; (3) alcohol and other drug use; (4) sexual behaviors related to unintended pregnancy and sexually transmitted infections (STIs), including human immunodeficiency virus (HIV) infection; (5) unhealthy dietary behaviors; and (6) physical inactivity. The purpose is to make the community at large aware of the prevalence of risky behaviors in high school students to provide educators and community members with information to guide their educational, prevention, and intervention efforts.

Those risk factors come with scary statistics. And we know the best way to stop an issue is to prevent it. Dr. Harvey Fineberg of John Hopkins Bloomberg School of Public Health discusses "The Paradox of Disease Prevention: Celebrated in Principle, Resisted in Practice." He demonstrates a few of the reasons that prevention is a hard sell in the medical field that we can also learn from in education (Fineberg, 2014).

One of the issues is that success is invisible. When your SEL practices are successful, you may not see a noticeable decline in behaviors for a while. And you may not be able to quantify the things that didn't happen. When a student makes a good choice through learning self-management or emotional regulation, we may never know. We are only aware when a student makes a bad choice.

TASK: Make success visible

Have active discussions with your students. Call it "the good choice I made today." Educators can have students journal or put the good decisions in a jar where you can read and discuss them once a week. Have students write an essay about a time when they had to make a good choice and what resources they had to make that choice.

For example, they had a friend to talk to about it, or they did a few deep breaths before speaking back to someone who was mean.

One example: One student I was talking to said out of the blue, "I get in a really bad mood after my last class of the day. I don't think my teacher likes me. I think I am going to try and work out after school so that mood doesn't ruin the rest of my day." It was thrilling to hear him work through that all on his own. He identified the emotions he was feeling, the cause of the emotions, and the way he planned to resolve them.

There is the prevention that we do not hear about. That student could have made a different decision in how he works through those emotions and feelings. He could have been rude to the teacher, skipped class, or blamed himself. But he didn't. That is why it is so important to teach, model, and practice social and emotional competencies for your students, and this could be your kid as well. Prevention is hard because it is invisible. Consider ways to make it visible in your school.

Making Prevention Compelling: Statistics Aren't Personal

People don't change their dental hygiene practice after hearing that four out of five dentists agree. And they haven't stopped the process of getting married after hearing that almost half of marriages end in divorce. The problem with statistics is that they aren't personal. They may tell a story, but it isn't your story, and it can be hard to connect with. Especially if the story is that something did NOT happen because of a specific practice.

Why are statistics not as compelling? We often use statistics to tell the prevention story. Statistics, as a science, is the collection, analysis, presentation, and interpretation of data. And statistics are critical to demonstrating the efficacy of an approach and describing it as evidence based. But connecting the evidence with statistical outcomes can be lacking.

This can be true when we work in promoting social emotional learning as well. We use the seminal meta-analysis (Durlak et al., 2011) to demonstrate the outcome that there was an 11 percentile–point gain in achievement among the 213 studies examined. But how can we make this applicable to our own story?

If you dig further into the meta-analysis, you will find that they used standardized reading or math achievement test scores and school grades (overall GPA or specific grades in math or reading). Academic performance from grades and test scores only improved when the teacher implemented programs that were evidence based and well-executed (Durlak et al., 2011).

To make social emotional learning and prevention, in general, live in your specific environment, we need to connect it to measurable, observable, and objective evidence and then have it tell your story. How did the implementation of SEL affect **your** student's GPA and test scores?

All schools are in the business of educational achievement. We can promote SEL as a tool to increase the capacity for teaching the necessary skills to be able to excel in an academic environment.

And your story can look like this:

At _____ school, we used the evidence-based SEL program _____.
We also implemented SEL into our daily teaching practices, our school culture, and our academic lessons. To prepare all teachers to implement SEL, we did

_____.

We then compared the test scores from before and after SEL implementation and we found _____. _____% more students made the honor roll and _____ received higher test scores. We also compared discipline referrals, suspensions, and bullying incidents and found a decrease by _____%.

Informational NOT Evaluative

I would like to make the point that this information should be used to understand the relationship between SEL and academic achievement and *not* be used as another evaluation tool against educators. We need to know what works and why. Getting there will take time. Many schools and districts are at the beginning of the process of SEL implementation. But before momentum wanes, as it often does in education, we need to develop ways to tell our unique story of prevention and outcomes that stakeholders can make personal.

Choosing Programs and Interventions

Your next step is to decide what SEL program or interventions to use to meet your goals. There are many evidence-based programs that require different types of resource use. Resource use means how much money, time, and training will be required by each program. For example, there are hundreds of social emotional learning books, programs, curricula, assessments, articles, speakers, consultants, and trainings. Your school will need to prioritize their needs and the outcomes that they want to achieve with the resources they have to invest in the program.

One of the key focuses of being an SEL coach is choosing the intervention you will use to create change. The intervention you choose should be directly tied to your outcomes. There are many evidence-based programs that have different levels of resource use.

Let's explore how to choose a program or intervention that meets the needs of your school. Which programs or interventions will you use to create meaningful change? The intervention you choose should be directly tied to the SEL goals and outcomes you set.

TASK: Create a process to determine which strategies, programs, interventions to try

Here are a few questions to help guide you when considering the best program for your school:

- Is the program developmentally appropriate?

- Is it evidence based?

- What's the cost?

- Who will be needed to support the administration of the program or intervention?

- Who will collect and interpret the data?

- What will you do with the data collected?

- How much time is needed?

- Will this fit into our schedule?

- How will outcomes be assessed?

These questions are essential to thinking through designing an SEL program that works for you. If schools choose not to evaluate their resources, they may experience an implementation gap due to the lack of clarity around what's possible. Part of adopting a new program or intervention is examining the interventions before attempting to implement them. As an SEL coach, you may be responsible for evaluating both new interventions and previous programs. There are many tools and resources that allow you to complete this task, including tools from CASEL (Collaborative for Academic, Social, and Emotional Learning) and Explore SEL from Harvard University. Examine the data you'll need to determine if a program or intervention is right for your school. Schools need to prioritize their needs and the outcomes that they want to obtain with the resources they have to take on the project.

Promoting Student Engagement

We need to intentionally think about how to invest students in demonstrating their own agency for their own needs. We have spent a lot of time in the past trying to "help" students without getting their input or talking to them about their perceptions of what would be helpful. With SEL we should move from doing things for students to more of doing things *with* students, allowing student input and a problem-solving process. We need to be in a partnership with students while supporting them in developing their own competencies.

Compliance is often used in educational systems to get students to do what we think is best for them. But compliance can go wrong because of the disciplinary actions that need to be in place if the student does not select to do what we are asking. When we are thinking about how to develop these crucial life skills, we need to think more about how to develop their interest and see the applicability in not only their academic goals but their personal ones as well. Our goal is to encourage engagement in the development of their own social and emotional competencies. How can we do that?

TASK: Determine strategies to promote student engagement

- Teach students about the difference between intrinsic and extrinsic motivation. Help them discover their own intrinsic motivators and connect them to the skills they need to achieve those goals.

- Ask them to think about how having a fixed or growth mindset can affect how we face any obstacle.

- Engage student input in how to learn, teach, grow, and develop these skills.

- Talk to students about making the most of the small moments, and give examples.

- Infuse relationship-building strategies throughout the year to help them give some of these strategies a chance, even if they can't see "why are we learning about this."

- Teach students about the pause button (a self-regulation technique) that allows students' brains not to get hijacked by automatic negative thinking.

PHASE 3: LEADERSHIP AND FACILITATOR ROLE TASKS

Braid Your Current Interventions to Determine Gaps

Another important strategy includes a process that aligns or braids together these interventions to demonstrate that our goal for teaching and promoting social emotional learning is just another piece to developing and preparing students for life outside of formal education. Academic knowledge and social emotional learning go hand in hand. Working together, students are given the skills to succeed in college and career, in relationships, and in community, and be resilient in the face of adversity. Each of these separate programs and processes should braid into a central vision for your school or district. These are the practices that produce the outcomes that fall under the vision that you see for the students at your school (Rogers, 2019).

Educational stakeholders should discuss the braiding of initiatives. What processes and procedures are you doing that look at how each initiative meets the varying needs at the school level? Are new initiatives coming up that contradict, add more to, replicate, or confuse what you are already doing? If so, work toward eliminating them. Can you integrate processes between PBIS (if currently used) and SEL? Between the problem-solving process and behavioral expectations? Between skill development through curriculum and schoolwide practices?

TASK: Braid your initiatives

BRAIDING EXAMPLE

VISION: (DISTRICT/SCHOOL OR INITIATIVE) VISION STATEMENT HERE
GOAL 1:
GOAL 2:
GOAL 3:

INITIATIVE, PROJECT, OR COMMITTEE	PURPOSE	ALIGNS WITH WHICH GOAL	TARGET GROUP	STAFF INVOLVED	OUTCOMES
SEL curriculum	Teachers will deliver the selected SEL curriculum to increase their students' social and emotional competencies.	Goal 1	All students	All staff	This school year all students received 20 SEL lessons. Competencies were measured through teacher reports.
Growth mindset book study					
Bullying education					
School improvement plans					

(Continued)

INITIATIVE, PROJECT, OR COMMITTEE	PURPOSE	ALIGNS WITH WHICH GOAL	TARGET GROUP	STAFF INVOLVED	OUTCOMES
PBIS (positive behavior interventions and supports)					
Academic curriculum					
School-based mental health services					
Afterschool programming					
MTSS/RTI					
College and career readiness					
Discipline practices					

The Process for Accessing Targeted Interventions

The system needs to avoid random acts of intervention. Targeted intervention, or Tier 2 interventions need to be determined by some type of standard. What process will your school use for determining who needs Tier 2 interventions? Why is it essential to have buy-in from a teacher for interventions? What data will be collected to support the need for Tier 2 interventions?

Hopefully, the case has been made here that until you have a solid foundation for your universal SEL practices, there should be no looking forward to Tier 2. But this will often be where schools and systems want to start because they are often the students who are exhibiting the most disruption in the day.

TASK: Create a process for Tier 2 (targeted) interventions and supports

To look ahead briefly, this is one way to create a process of what should be put in place prior to having a student access Tier 2 supports.

1. Staff requests help with student/s.

2. Inquire: What have you tried? Is there anything that has worked, even for a small period?

3. After informal consultation (e.g., hallway stop), if behavior repeats or escalates AND it is determined that a lack of universal social and emotional competencies is the cause, have a formal meeting.

4. At the formal meeting, write notes about concerns from meeting.

5. Do a third-party (SEL coach, dean, counselor, educational stakeholders, etc.) observation and data collection.

6. Proceed with consultation conversation with the teacher about data collected and suggestions for universal intervention if appropriate (may move directly to Tier 2 or 3 depending on the severity of behaviors present).

7. Select universal intervention (whole class).

8. Perform evidence-based practice: teaching/reminding/modeling etc.

9. Do progress monitoring: the SEL coach will help set up and the teacher collects data to demonstrate if the intervention is working.

10. Within a predetermined timeline, check for fidelity of implementation (SEL coach with the teacher).

11. Use data-based decision-making to determine next steps: continue with universal, alter the intervention, move to Tier 2, stop intervention, try something else.

12. If determined that Tier 2 is the next best course, give teachers an understanding of available Tier 2 supports, and hold a Tier 2 meeting with all appropriate staff.

Enhance Student Voice Through a Youth Advisory Board

To invite students into the decision-making process, stakeholders may want to create a youth advisory board. This group should be formed with the same care and consideration that you use in forming the teams at school. Diverse members of students should participate. This is a leadership opportunity where students can provide guidance on the wording of surveys that are going out from the school, feedback on specific lessons or practices that focus on equity, and/or analysis of the data that directly affects them, and provide solutions that they and their peers buy into.

Leadership will want to decide and set the expectation for the things that students will and will not have a choice in this process. Setting the expectation about the purpose of the group and what sort of decisions they will be able to make is vital. Students do not want to waste their time on this work if it is just a meaningless exercise where no real change that they suggest will be accepted. Make their work meaningful and they will continue to be invested in the process.

Create a youth advisory board

1. Decide on the purpose of the group:

   a. guidance on student engagement and participation

   b. feedback on specific SEL lessons

   c. practices that focus on equity

   d. leading community service efforts

   e. other?

2. Use meeting schedule.

3. Determine the objective, activity, and prep in collaboration with students.

4. Measure outcomes/use of recommendations from the youth advisory board.

Youth Advisory Board Planning Schedule (example)

INTRO	OBJECTIVE	ACTIVITY	PREP
Meeting 1	Leadership inventory and styles; leadership roles		
Meeting 2	Leadership challenge—think of a problem: at school, locally, globally		
Meeting 3	Developing creative solutions that can work		
Meeting 4	Action plan/Goals		
Meeting 5	How does a leader solve problems?		
Meeting 6	Planning for event		
Meeting 7	Planning for event		
Meeting 8	Assess planning/Did we reach our goal?		

Creating an Intervention Matrix

Another process to engage in is determining the skills that students are missing or need to develop. An intervention matrix will help teachers and other educators to identify behaviors that exemplify a need for training or skill development. For example, if we see that students are having issues with dealing with gossip, we might want to develop their social awareness competencies.

An intervention matrix looks at the behaviors and skills and matches them to areas of need. In the example that follows, the developmentally appropriate competencies were linked using a state competency matrix, in this case, Wisconsin's (https://dpi.wi.gov/sspw/mental-health/social-emotional-learning/competencies). SEL coaches can use this to determine the exact skills that students need or are having difficulty or an inability to demonstrate. This more closely aligns with the specific interventions that you would like to use in your building. The SEL team can work on this for your school or district to determine what the "look fors" for each skill development needs to be. We often administer SEL programs or practices without first determining what specific skills our students could benefit from the most. This process allows you to move closer to the goal of providing students with the specific skills that they need and will benefit them the most.

The following are examples of using developmental milestones for social and emotional competencies.

Example

AGE OF STUDENT	STUDENT CAN:	STUDENT NEEDS:	SKILL BUILDING:	COMPETENCY
1st–3rd grade	Learners will be able to identify and describe skills and activities they do well and those for which they need help.	Inability or difficulty with: • Talking about what they are good at • Talking about what they need help with • Asking for help • Knowing who they can ask for help	• Describe skills they are good at • Describe activities they do well • Describe times when they need help • Describe how they can ask for help • Determine who would be best to ask for help	Self-awareness
4th–5th grade	Learners will be able to effectively communicate clearly, listen well, and cooperate with others to build healthy relationships.	Inability or difficulty with: • Communicating • Listening to others • Cooperating with friends and classmates	• How to talk to others • How to listen to others • How to advocate for themselves in meaningful ways • Working together for one goal • Understanding fair practices • Discover others' needs and wants	Relationship skills
6th–8th grade	Learners will be able to identify what stressors create strong emotion and apply an appropriate calming or coping strategy to defuse the emotional trigger.	Inability or difficulty with: • Labeling what makes them upset • Knowing when to use strategies to calm self • Knowing how to calm self through thoughts or actions	• Identify triggers • Use calming strategies • Develop coping strategies	Self-management

(Continued)

(Continued)

AGE OF STUDENT	STUDENT CAN:	STUDENT NEEDS:	SKILL BUILDING:	COMPETENCY
		• Asking for the help using social support		
9th–10th grade	Learners will be able to demonstrate empathy to others who have different views and beliefs.	Inability or difficulty with: • Showing that they understand the difference between their feelings and others • Verbalizing how someone else may feel • Understanding why others may have different views or beliefs	• Discuss how others feel • Develop the ability to tell the differences in thoughts, beliefs, and views between others and own • Put themselves in another person's shoes • Speak to others' views and beliefs	Social awareness
11th grade–adult	Learners will be able to consider a variety of factors (e.g., ethical, safety, and societal factors) to make decisions that promote productive social and work relations.	Inability or difficulty with: • Keeping multiple concepts in flux • Being aware of ethical issues • Knowing safe behaviors • Being aware of social norms • Decision-making • Making choices that promote positive personal relationships • Making choices that promote positive working relationships	• Ethical reasoning • Understanding safety considerations • Learn about relevant societal factors • Problem-solving process • Evaluating possible decisions to choose the most responsible one	Responsible decision-making

PHASE 4: LEADERSHIP AND FACILITATOR ROLE TASKS

Year at a Glance

A year-at-a-glance document can be a great way to plan and prepare for the school year. It is a part of your planner that lists all the upcoming events throughout the year. The year at a glance helps you see a high-level view of what your year might look like. It not only helps you to understand what needs to be scheduled month to month but also what you hope to accomplish in the year.

TASK: Create a year at a glance

EXAMPLE:	SOCIAL EMOTIONAL LEARNING COACH/LEAD IMPLEMENTER YEAR AT A GLANCE

Before school starts	• Inform staff of role and promote vision and goals
	• Meet with the SEL team and add new members as needed
	• Update website with personal info
	• Meet with principal to discuss
	  ○ schedule in building
	  ○ status of the SEL team and other teams in building
	  ○ office space
	  ○ meeting schedule at the district
	  ○ schedule PD and other related dates for the year
	  ○ action plan
	• Review tiered inventory notebook for your building
	• Determine data collection plan
	• Begin self-care planning for staff
	• Review all available resources
	• Schedule staff training time with the principal about training times
	• Connected to all necessary tech

September	• Support with transition needs in the first week of school • Administer and collect belief surveys • Schedule observation with supervisor • Newsletter • Meet with the SEL team • Review universal implementation • Create a tracking system for observations, teacher meetings, student interventions • Establish a system for teachers to request support or observations

(Continued)

(Continued)

EXAMPLE:	SOCIAL EMOTIONAL LEARNING COACH/LEAD IMPLEMENTER YEAR AT A GLANCE
October	• Newsletter • Meet with the SEL team • Schedule observation with SEL supervisor • Share survey results PD with staff • Administer universal screener (building determined) • Parent night
November	• Schedule observation with supervisor • Newsletter • Meet with the SEL team • Outside training or conference (tentative) • Review school climate data
December	• Newsletter • Meet with the SEL team • Support parent conferences
January	• Schedule observation with SEL supervisor • Newsletter • Meet with the SEL team • Set coaching observations after the break
February	• Schedule observation with SEL supervisor • Newsletter • Meet with the SEL team • Administer universal screener (building determined) • Self-care PD • Coaching clinics
March	• Schedule observation with SEL supervisor • Newsletter • Meet with the SEL team • Parent night • Assess data tracking system

EXAMPLE:	SOCIAL EMOTIONAL LEARNING COACH/LEAD IMPLEMENTER YEAR AT A GLANCE
April	• Schedule observation with SEL supervisor • Newsletter • Meet with the SEL team • Coaching clinics
May	• Schedule observation with SEL supervisor • Newsletter • Meet with the SEL team • Self-care reminders
June	• Tiered intervention inventory notebooks are due • Newsletter • Meet with the SEL team • Yearly SEL reflections (staff and team)
After school is out	• Year-end coach reflections • Organization of Google docs

Creating a Universal Intervention Manual

Change agents should consider what this intervention/program/process looks like in your school or district. Create a document that reflects your practices that serve your implementation. As previously discussed, context is vital in determining how the intervention will work. Producing a manual that explains the process to anyone who is new to the system will be one of the quickest ways to bring new people on board.

A manual is a great introduction to the intervention for all stakeholders, especially those who are new to your building or culture. Begin by asking yourself what your process is. How do you go about your social emotional learning instruction? What procedures can be manualized so that new teachers do not have to reinvent the wheel?

Include information about innovative procedures during implementation. Some examples could include the following:

- Monthly themes
- Educational assistant/paraprofessional specific trainings
- Teachable moments
- Application in the dean or principal's office
- Problem-solving for recess attendants
- Training for classified staff: bus drivers, secretaries, lunchroom staff
- Books used to discuss social and emotional skills
- Videos created or used during implementation
- Tier 2 or 3 (small group or individual) use of SEL

Sections to include in the universal manual

Table of Contents

UNIVERSAL PROCESS	PAGE #
Problem-solving process (universal)	3
Matching interventions to social emotional competencies	4
Observation form (pre-intervention)	7
Observation form (after intervention selected and implemented)	8
UNIVERSAL INTERVENTIONS	
Procedures for morning meeting	9–11
Books with SEL themes (by grade)	12–13
Writing prompts for SEL topics	14
Classroom needs assessment	15–18
Brain breaks	19
Procedures for optimistic closure	20
Demonstrating warmth and support	21–24
Engagement practices	25
Identifying stressors	26
Building relationships throughout the school year	27
Teach, model, and reinforce prosocial skills	28–29
Emotion planning	30–31
Goal mapping	32
Gratitude practice	33–35
Deep listening practices	36–37
Mind Jar	38

Example of lesson in universal implementation manual

TEACH PROSOCIAL SKILLS ELEMENTARY AND SECONDARY	
Objective	• To increase on-task, expected behaviors • To make students identify good behavior • To help reinforce character development • To create a climate of respect • To make it more meaningful to students than teacher-imposed rules • To verbalize and internalize appropriate behavior • To set standards for cooperative groups (team tasks) and develop social skills
Prep	• Choose a social skill (e.g., respect, cooperation, responsibility). Or choose a routine/activity (e.g., a lesson on the carpet, independent work time, peer conference). • Get a piece of **yellow** chart paper and markers.
Teaching/ Planning	1. Gather the class on the carpet. Use yellow chart paper to create a T-graph. 2. **"What does _____ (e.g., cooperation) mean?"** Call on a few hands and record their thoughts on the top of the yellow chart paper. 3. **"What will we see in our classroom when students are (cooperating)_____? Turn and talk."** Give students 1 minute to talk, then call on several hands and record their words in the "See" column on the chart. 4. **"What will we hear in our classroom when students are (cooperating) _____? Turn and talk."** Give students 1 minute to talk, then call on several hands and record their words in the "hear" column on the chart. 5. **"I will be awarding team points when I notice table groups showing _____."** **For the next 3–4 weeks:** • Revisit the T-graph often with students to add behaviors that have been observed (in a different color). • When you notice a student/table group demonstrating the skill, say things like **"Thank your blue group for taking turns talking." "I like how someone in the red group said, 'Can you please help me?' when they were stuck."** Award A LOT of team points this way. • Have teams set a goal (e.g., the purple group may decide that they're going to focus on "taking turns" from the "see" side of the t-graph).
Follow Through and Reminders	• Give students specific, positive praise by recognizing and naming when they demonstrate the behaviors/language on the T-graph.

How to create write-up intervention templates

Step 1: Review each intervention that you have found works in your system.

Step 2: Determine if there are any questions or additions to the intervention. Do any of the ideas need further clarification?

Step 3: Create implementation instructions and include evidence-based practices. Consider using SAFE (sustained, active, frequent, and explicit) as a guideline. Use the aforementioned template or any other that makes sense for your school.

Step 4: Create an observation form for progress monitoring for the intervention.

Step 5: Put all materials together and distribute them to educational stakeholders.

Organize Materials for Ease of Use

Keeping a notebook of all your materials is a best practice. If you would prefer and it feels more helpful, use OneNote or Google Docs to keep everything together. You will collect different types of forms and data. This can include meeting notes, data used during your SEL team meetings and staff trainings, staff feedback, notes from teacher observations, emails from teachers (especially complimentary ones), how many times you met with teachers, and the results of meetings (as well as next steps). Include anything that will help you construct a narrative that tells you where you started, what you did, and where you ended year over year. For example, you may have journal articles, materials from different schools and districts that you could use as examples or templates. Examples of SEL standards from your state and/or other states, SEL lessons and PD samples that you have used in the past, and implementation for each of the skills. Parent resources, staff newsletters, and teacher reflections on practice can also be useful.

TASK: Collect and organize resources

One of the challenges in SEL implementation is keeping track of the many types of resources available in your work. It will require stretching your organizational skills to have the information that you need ready and easy to find when you need it.

Got It/No Thanks/Need It

Please go through this list. The items may have multiple markers.

(Continued)

(Continued)

Key

Items that you have, highlight green.

Items that you don't have and don't want to, highlight yellow.

Items that you need because you don't have, highlight red.

Items that you want to talk about, make bold and underline.

Items that you have used, add three asterisks.

Resources

- 2-minute countdown for helping students prepare for the end of class

- Tiered interventions (specific to school) document

- Whole class contingency classroom management system

- Home/school communication

- Goal-setting form

- Rita Pierson Ted Talk

- Picture books about behavior, social emotional situations

- Connect and collaborate Google form

- Post-meeting and PD evaluation Google forms

- Empathy YouTube

- 8 ways to build positive relationships: article

- Motivational videos

- Transitions interventions

- Student reflections (classroom teacher)

- Setting the stage for positive behaviors

- Student observation rating form

- Daily organization checklist

- The science of happiness: gratitude video

- Difficult conversations discussion guide/key points/worksheet

- Video about five CASEL competencies: https://bit.ly/3loWVd5

- Brené Brown/parent perspective/Daring Greatly

- Neuroscience and SEL: https://bit.ly/3sKTjGr

- The economic value of social and emotional learning (benefit-cost studies)

- Ideas and tools for working with parents and family

- SEL: 10 things you can do at home

- Books for educators and parents

CAROLINE CHASE

SEL Consultant, Retired Assistant Director of SEL

Texas

Interview:

1. *What have you learned from being a part of a large district rollout?*

   I have done some heavy, long thinking about how our system does not handle adult SEL in a way that really promotes SEL because adults think they are already put together and none of us are. My grandma used to tell me that we all keep growing and changing until our last breath. That is truly my philosophy about SEL, and what is happening at the leadership level is the antithesis of that. The contradiction that, I'm in it, I've got it, yet you have people who are yelling at their employees.

2. *What did you find was most effective about the program or practice that you did specifically related to SEL implementation?*

   We rolled it out by vertical team: a high school and all of the elementary and middle schools that make up its feeder pattern.

What we did, in the beginning, is we decided we would roll it out over five years. That was the goal. And we invited our vertical team leaders to talk to their staff and see if they were interested in piloting the first year. We had done a little pilot in the year 2010 before we actually formed the department with three elementary schools. And we were going to take on two vertical teams that first year. Every year after that, we would add on two or three vertical teams until we had all 12. It was voluntary, and there was no mandate. There were things that you had to agree to do. One of them was to implement a curriculum pre-K through 8th grade depending on their school level. At the high school level, the two principals said we are not going to start any kind of teaching with students until y'all work with our adults. So, they were the ones who really worked with our teams. I will never forget when an assistant principal said to me, "I am sick and tired of grown adults coming to me and complaining about a colleague and then I asked them, 'Well what happened when you talked to this person about what's bothering you?' and they said, 'I didn't talk to them; I want you to fix this.' We have to get people to the point where they can resolve their own conflicts together in a peaceful way and model for these kids what we are hoping they will learn."

And so, that was the beginning for us in terms of how we figured out what is adult SEL and how do we approach this with teachers without insulting them? Because I go back to the idea that everybody thinks they're already put together. So we did some different things with them. We did a training with all the different campuses, and we asked all the principals to be at the training, and we asked them to put together a core SEL team on their campus and those folks would come as well. We had around six to eight people from each campus and we did a two-day training during the summer before they started implementing. We created tools for them to do a condensed training from what they learned for their staff. We created PowerPoints and all the notes and talking points, etc., knowing that there weren't enough of us to train every single school. And they were going to have to turn it around.

I'll tell you what really worked for us was that we hired people from the beginning who already had a reputation in the school district. One of my colleagues was one of the behavioral specialists I worked with in the past. Because of our prior work, we had touched on different campuses and it just so happened that the campuses that came on board, in the beginning, were many of the campuses that she and I had worked with already. So, there was some familiarity there and some established relationships that really helped start us on the right foot. Our biggest goal was to build relationships, build relationships. We had zero access to our principals as a group, as a whole group. It took us five years to finally get in front of all of the principals and be able to really work with them as leaders. It was something that was super frustrating because what we discovered was that we could never reach every one of them and they are key to the success of SEL in schools. We knew we couldn't just work with teachers because we couldn't reach every one of them. One of the things we did too—I think this is important—we did not put this on the counselors, and we didn't isolate certain teachers to do the lessons. We bought the curriculum kits for every teacher because we thought if they don't know the content, how they will reinforce the skill acquisition beyond doing one 30-minute lesson a week? How do students learn skills if we don't reinforce them? The counselors got a kit, and they were able to do the follow-up lessons or reinforcement lessons in a smaller group and that freed them up to do Tier 2 and Tier 3 work instead of trying to do SEL lessons for every classroom.

3. And how did you do that?

What was really helpful is that we just kept showing up. In the beginning, the most effective thing that we did in spite of times when we felt not really invited onto campus or they were suspicious about what we were doing because: here is more central office staff coming. We would show up and volunteer in the lunchroom at breakfast or at lunch. We would help with bus duty. We would hang out and just talk to teachers in the teacher workroom. We would ask if we could come in and just observe in a class to see what SEL practices the teachers were already engaged in well and leave notes highlighting SEL practices we saw in action in their classrooms. Because we knew the teachers, almost intuitively, were doing this work. The difference is that SEL makes it very explicit. So, relationship building was absolutely key, building trust fast, and then we got to the point where we started developing really helpful systems. And one of those things was asking campuses to develop an SEL steering committee. It was made up of people who were representative of the entire campus. And we wanted them to include an administrator because we did not want to have them go off in left field, and create some amazing idea just to be told, well we can't do that. We wanted someone there with a little bit of power, decision-making power. The lead of the steering committee was an SEL facilitator on every campus who was designated by the principal. That person and the steering committee did the work. We didn't want this to rest on any one person because when you make things person-centered if that person leaves, everything falls apart. Buy-in from the larger group was really important, and the schools were really good about doing that. As coaches, we helped the SEL facilitators on the campus understand how to run a meeting through an SEL lens as well as develop goals and action plans for their work based on campus data.

4. What helped with principal buy-in?

Eventually, when we did get in front of the principals, we taught them about the SEL 3 Signature Practices from CASEL. That was a *game-changer. I don't know what it was about that. Maybe its efficacy was because it was so simple and they could understand how they could use it in meetings or they could implement it in faculty meetings. These practices can be integrated into the classroom, in any format that made sense for opportunities for people to come together and learn more about each other and be able to process whatever information was being delivered. It was amazing. They just started using it almost immediately and it really shifted the culture of our whole district. Even the superintendent started dabbling in it and using it in his meetings with all of the principals that he has once a month. It was very important to refer back to the definition of SEL which states that this work is a process. It takes time, and has a foundation of explicit instruction, building a positive climate and culture, integrating SEL into academics, and involving families. Those were some things that were very, very, effective.*

5. *What was not effective?*

   One thing that was not effective in my opinion, and I think in a lot of people's opinions, was that we chose one instructional resource. We told everybody, "This is what you are going to use." We gave them training on it and it was super easy to use. But those lessons did not speak to all of our kids. We came to regret that decision because we realized we should have spent a lot more time up front on adult SEL. What we started doing was giving teachers permission to adapt those lessons to their students' reality. We encouraged them to focus on the concepts rather than sending the message that you must watch this video or you must do this activity in this way. We wanted them to try to get their kids to talk about the concepts in depth and relate those concepts to their own lives.

6. *What were the skills you had to have to do the work of SEL implementation? Where and how did you learn those skills?*

   Because we all enter into the work of SEL with our unique set of skills and competencies, it is imperative that we take a deep dive into all five competencies and skill sets to ascertain where we are in our own learning before we start to work with others. One doesn't have to "master" all the skills to do the work, but it is important to assess one's own strengths and areas of growth. The skills I had to lean on the most were: listening, perspective-taking, awareness of my own values and biases, inviting the perspectives of others into conversations and planning for SEL, and the ability to approach conflict with curiosity rather than apprehension. The ability to avoid personalizing others' criticisms or judgments about the work was extremely important as well. Personalizing often leads to defensiveness, which can shut down a conversation that can help bring people TO the work rather than pushing them away for their lack of "buy-in."

7. *When you think of the future of social emotional learning in your system or your work, what gives you a sense of hope? What makes you concerned or worried?*

   I am hopeful because I see an almost universal awareness of SEL and its value for humanity as we continue to move into the future. The pandemic and the social reckoning we are undergoing as a nation have brought this value to the forefront as all people are struggling with the changes that have occurred during this period of time. I am worried because we are divided as a people on how we should move forward, and we still don't have the SEL skill sets to be able to listen with curiosity to differences of opinion / ideology. There has also been so much added on to what began as Tier 1 SEL (equity, CP&I, trauma-informed practices, restorative practices, MTSS, etc.) that the SEL purist in me is concerned that social and emotional learning is being lost in the sea of acronyms. Proactive practices are a way to approach this work; they are not the work in and of itself.

CHAPTER 5

....

ADVANCE YOUR PRACTICE

Creating Teams That Work

Being a team member or team leader for your SEL work is one of the most important roles. SEL coaches should model shared leadership. The hope is that the coach will be able to bond tightly with the team and have monthly meetings with attainable goals where plans are developed and followed through. It is important to have an organized agenda and feedback to drive the next meeting and agenda.

PHASE 1: SEL TEAM ROLE TASKS

Developing a Team

Creating and developing teams are the most important tasks that an SEL coach will oversee. Meetings should be less about sit-and-get and more about a mutual exchange of ideas, thoughts, experiments, and project feedback. Each team member should be able to discuss with educational stakeholders what SEL is and is not. They need to feel comfortable with talking to their colleagues and getting to understand their perspectives. They will often be the voice of their grade level or subject area. So, it is important to speak positively about SEL when in other team meetings. They must also be comfortable in sharing their own experience and be open to listening to others with alternative ways of seeing an issue or situation.

Training your SEL teams will be an opportunity for you to learn more about SEL. In that meeting, you will learn more about universal interventions, understand the team-initiated problem-solving process, and learn how data can drive your action plan for SEL implementation at your school. Ideally, schools can learn from other schools and work together to create an action plan. It is important to offer opportunities for schoolwide action planning for the whole team.

You may wonder how many times the SEL team should meet in the school year. On average, the systems that I work with have nine meetings a year. The minimum number of times that teams met was 6 and the maximum was 16. It will be up to your system to determine the ideal time. But minimally, to move the work forward, plan for one whole team meeting a month, with communication via email and in person throughout the month.

TASK: Creating a team

Engage diverse stakeholders for a team:

- building administrators
- teachers (grade level, content or subject matter, special education, specialists)
- counselors
- school psychologists
- social workers
- librarians
- classified staff (secretary, student resource officers, lunch staff)
- paraprofessionals or educational assistants

Once a team has been solidified and team members feel comfortable with their understanding of SEL and implementation, the SEL team should expand to include parents or guardians, students, and even community members.

SEL Team Roles

All team members should be able to recommend items for the agenda and areas of need and analyze or interpret data to determine what the problem areas are. Every member needs to be an active participant. You should also consider a backup for each role. It is encouraged to NOT have the administrator play a primary role as facilitator, data analyst, or minute taker. Administrators need to be flexible with what might come up, and it is unpredictable when a situation causes administrator absence from a planned meeting. Since we know that this might occur, avoid the issue and set up the roles so that the team is not dependent on administrators being at the full meetings 100% of the time.

General Shared Commitments

These teams should be chosen specifically with faculty who will cheerlead this change. They are well-respected in the building and not afraid to be the first ones to try new things. These are your early adopters, and they will help guide the work within the building.

Consider: Who would like to take on each of these roles? Are they rotating or stable over the school year?

- Team lead = begins meeting and keeps structure through the agenda, makes sure all team members have a voice

- Notetaker = creates agenda and sends it out to team members before the meeting

- Data analyst = brings applicable data for the team to review, provides updates about the status of previous data and its use

- Timekeeper = monitors the use of time during the meeting to make sure that all agenda items are covered during the meeting

- Communicator = speaks with educational stakeholders about what the team is doing, goals, and is open to suggestions from others

The purpose of the school team is to use data/assessments to determine building needs, set priorities and monitor practices within the school, identify schoolwide strategies, staff training, and resources, oversee program implementation, and share team goals and outcomes within the building.

Make sure that your team can discuss and elaborate on your purpose. Can they speak to others about what your change is about? Do they have an elevator speech? Everyone on the team should be able to talk about the benefits of your program or process. **Make sure that they have an answer to the question, What's in it for me?**

TASK: Things to consider for creating shared commitments

- How will team members communicate?

- How will decisions be made? Will there have to be outside agreement by other parties who are not on the team?

- What will the expectations be for team members' interactions during meetings?

- What method will the team use to solve problems and resolve conflict?

- How would responsibilities be decided and kept accountable for individuals assigned the task?

- What are the expectations in an online environment that is teaming? Regular attendance? Return time for emails?

Norms for Practice

This is often a step we want to skip because we use teaming so often in education. I would recommend selecting norms because this team is so unique in its approach, and I ask that you form a group that will support your SEL implementation.

Norms could include the following:

- Be open to continuous learning and others' perspectives, ideas, and styles.

- Respect the time of others (come on time, be prepared).

- Ask for help when needed.

- Respect colleagues by providing feedback directly to the person involved.

- Maintain confidentiality about district staff, students, and families.

- Self-regulate sharing to 3 minutes.

- Work as a team (in it together).

- Respectfully speak your truth.

- Stay engaged.

- Follow the agenda.

- Set an intention before talking.

- No side conversations.

- Listen attentively.

- Monitor your airtime.

- Take turns talking.

- Be kind.

- Avoid interrupting others when they are speaking.

- Address schoolwide issues and not individual student concerns.

- Conduct team business in front of the group.

- Be open and considerate to different viewpoints and ideas.

- Come prepared with team input when needed for meetings.

Discussion template:

1. Give members individual think time for considering past meetings and groups that they have been a part of to choose norms that they find particularly meaningful.

2. Have the group share the norms that they want to put up for consideration.

3. Have a discussion to determine which norms make the most sense for this group and eliminate overlap.

4. Vote on four to seven norms for the SEL team.

5. Implement the teams and review them regularly. Include them on every agenda.

Agendas That Work

You are most likely familiar with agendas in your work. This agenda is for a two-hour working meeting that has a specific intent to help the team develop materials and ideas that will forward your SEL implementation. In this sample, notice that the agenda is brief. This allows for focus on work. You will want to allow everyone to contribute an agenda item and send the agenda to every team member before the meeting.

TASK: Create an agenda that includes

1. List of expected attendees including guests that can be also used as roll call

2. Date, time, and location, and it should be sent out in advance of the meeting so the members can prepare

3. Norms on every agenda

4. Itemized list that includes time, brief description, and the owner or leader of that segment of time

5. A check-in that everyone can choose to participate in. For example, V = vent, S = share, or C = compliment

6. Color code agenda
   - Yellow = topic the group has been working on
   - Green = new topic, the focus of the meeting
   - Red = next steps of the plan (include who and when)

SEL Team Meeting Sample

Attendees

- Jennifer Rogers
- Manuel Rios
- Libby Estes
- Joe Westinghouse

Date: _____

Time: _____

Location: _____

Norms:

1. Follow the agenda

2. Keep discussions from our meetings confidential

3. Assume positive intent

4. Set an intention before talking

5. Follow the chain of command

6. Be a good listener

7. Respect different sharing styles

TIME	ITEM	OWNER
9:00	Check-in with intention: vent, share, celebrate	Jennifer
9:15	Next steps (parent workshop planning)	Manuel
9:30	Today: Review school climate data in the SEL plan	Workgroups
10:15	Share our findings	Workgroups
10:45	Priorities based on findings	Team
11:00	Assignments and adjournment	Jennifer

. . . .

80   THE SEL COACH

SEL Team Meeting Minutes: Example

After each meeting, there should be a record of the minutes of the meeting. It can include topics, discussions/takeaways, and action items. Team meeting minutes are the documents that describe what you did and why. It keeps your SEL team accountable and helps to prevent things from falling off the radar. And over time it will tell the story of your SEL implementation.

TASK: Adopt an SEL team meeting minutes document

SEL Team Meeting Minutes

Date:	Note Taker:
Attendees:	Timekeeper:

MEETING AGENDA	
Topic	**Discussion/Take-Aways**
Parent/Family Night PPT Review and Planning	• Team members who worked on the four main parts of the PPT presented their slides. Team members gave feedback on content and formatting. • Slides will be updated and shared with the coaches. • Middle school presentations are scheduled from 6:30 p.m. to 8:00 p.m.
Group Planning Time	• Team members met in presentation groups to plan their presentations. • Sections of the PowerPoint were assigned to individual team members to present.
Leveraging Your Time	• Supervisors will meet with team members individually to look at daily schedules and identify a time management strategy.

(Continued)

(Continued)

ACTION ITEMS		
Task	**Who Is Responsible**	**Timeline**
Review your section of the parent night PowerPoint presentation. Contact for any questions.	All team members	Before your parent night is scheduled

PARKING LOT/TOPICS TO COVER FOR NEXT MEETING

Introducing the Team

It is important to introduce the SEL team to the staff. This can be in a short succinct way that is meaningful. Teachers and staff should walk away with an understanding of what the SEL team is there to do and not do and how they can be useful in helping them. You may decide to speak briefly about the team goals and how they work with the overall goal of the school or district. But make sure to focus particularly on the benefits as they relate to their work with teachers.

TASK: Plan for introducing team and purpose to other stakeholders

Determine the best way to introduce the team members and discuss the purpose of the SEL team including goals for the year. The administration may choose to introduce the team in a staff meeting, email, and/or on the school website. Address the following questions:

1. What can the SEL team do to help the staff?

2. What can you expect from the team?

3. How can staff communicate with the SEL team?

One school I worked with found it helpful to create one email address that went to all team members. This way everyone was receiving the same information and kept the communication consistent between members.

PHASE 2: SEL TEAM ROLE TASKS

Consensus Practices

As mentioned in *Leading for Change Through Whole School Social Emotional Learning*, a consensus is crucial when teaming. Staff consensus does not necessarily mean that everyone agrees. Formal consensus procedures work well in systems where the expectation is that we work together but we may not always agree. These procedures help stakeholders work together to find a mutually acceptable solution. If your school does not practice consensus-based decision-making, it may be worth considering. It can help with the process of determining a vision for your work. And it can be used at many other decision points during the implementation of social emotional learning (Rogers, 2019).

The SEL team will need to create a way to quickly make decisions and understand where everyone sits on specific decisions.

There are levels of consensus:

1. I can say an unqualified "yes."

2. I can accept the decision.

3. I can live with the decision.

4. I do not fully agree with the decision; however, I will not block it and will support it.

5. I refuse to enter consensus.

Do we want the fourth level of consensus as our typical response? It isn't ideal, but we have to expect in a school with a variety of personalities, this will happen. If you have more than one member who strongly believes that this is the wrong thing to do and refuses to enter consensus, it is time to take a pause. At that point, it will be a good idea to try and understand the point of view of the dissenting members. They may be your canary in the coal mine. It may require more negotiation to get to a point where true consensus can be achieved (Rogers, 2019).

The Feedback Flow Between the Coach and Team

You may discuss how communication is ideally structured with this feedback flow. Why do we do this? To increase understanding of the process/product and to encourage stakeholders to voice concerns and remedy as much pushback as possible. For example, your staff has requested an easy-to-use stress management technique for use with their students. You may work with the team to think through potential issues before pushing it out to the whole staff.

TASK: Create a flow process for the communications and strategies with team input

The process might be helpful to design something with team input.

1. Coach asks a procedural question to staff getting input from all appropriate stakeholders.

2. Coach uses the information to create themes and gives direction to the product.

3. Coach creates a template.

4. The team gives feedback on the template.

5. Coach tweaks document or product.

6. The team gives approval.

7. Coach gets administration buy-in (if not part of the team).

8. Coach proceeds with dissemination and education to appropriate staff.

9. Coach receives feedback from staff about applicability, timeliness, and usefulness.

10. Coach and team tweaks again if necessary.

Motivating a Team

With everything that is going on at school, there may be times when your team is not motivated. It will be the SEL coaches' responsibility to plan for that. Some ideas to motivate your team are as follows:

- Provide opportunities for the members to get to know each other and bond with one another.

- Let your team members know that you value them and that each member will have a different skill set that is needed for your overall success.

- Take their input and suggestions seriously. If they are not feasible, explain why they might not work.

- Celebrate small wins.

- Clarify goals and identify how progress toward the goals is happening.

- Be on their side.

- Include them in building solutions to common problems.

TASK: Plan for ways to motivate your team

Reflect on the following:

- What do you know about the team members?

- What do you need to know?

- What motivates them?

- How can you integrate their motivations into your SEL implementation?

Maintaining an SEL Team

Maintaining an SEL team year over year can be a challenge. Do you have the same people participating to create continuity and a deeper understanding of SEL and what has been done during implementation? Or do you incorporate new members every year who can add different perspectives to the work? These will have to be personal decisions for your school's unique characteristics. There are pros and cons to each way of looking at the longevity of the team. The important question to ask is how your SEL team is functioning. Are you able to work together effectively? Are your goals being accomplished through the current structure of the team? Consider these questions as the SEL coach with administration and the team.

TASK: How is your team functioning? Do you need to change it?

Reflection on the SEL team:

- How does the SEL team currently manage decision-making?

- How does your SEL team create goals?

- What is the consensus process like?

- Are there members who cannot commit to following the norms for meetings?

- Are there members who are finding it hard to make the commitment to attend and participate in the meetings as they once did?

- Are all the members communicating well?

- If we were to change one thing about the team as it is currently, what would that be?

- If we are to keep the current members, what is one thing we need to change moving forward?

Recruit and Train New Members of the Team

There may be times when the team numbers diminish because of people leaving the school or retiring. There may be other interventions or teams that the members would like to be a part of. Or there may just be a mutual parting of the ways for team members. It is natural to have ebbs and flows of individuals on teams. The SEL coach would benefit from understanding and preparing for this. They may want to consider how they can leverage their relationships with other staff members to ask if they would like to participate. Talk to the SEL team to see if there is someone they would recommend joining the team.

To get the new team members up to speed, the SEL coach may need to think about how to train them.

Consider the following:

- Why were they recruited? What are their skill sets? And once you know that, ask them to fill a role that will match the need on the team.

- How can the other SEL team members help get the new members up to speed?

- Giving them access to previous agendas and meeting minutes, notes, or presentations that the team has created in the past.

- Determine what specific skills they need to be a beneficial part of the team and train them in those areas first.

PHASE 3: SEL TEAM SUPPORT ROLE TASKS

Team Data Analysis

Use a problem-solving process to determine the direction of your universal SEL efforts—a way to determine your focus based on your specific needs. Data collection and analysis drive the next steps in our SEL work. Use data to drive your decisions systemically and with individual students and scenarios. Looking at systemic data may involve a multistep process that looks at different parts of the problem and tries to solve for all the parts. This information can be collected to see if there are specific problems that you are seeing schoolwide, to design trainings for specific SEL strategies that are regularly used, and/or to determine which curriculum to purchase based on student SEL competency needs. Using a process will help determine how teams can create and lead PD, how to select appropriate interventions, and how to action plan. The team can also analyze data to determine how it informs your action plan. Design a plan to help educators with a way to look at data.

TASK: Questions for the team to think through when working with data

- Where did the data come from? What was it meant to measure? How long ago was the data collected?

- What does the data tell us? What can the data not tell us?

- What patterns/trends do we see in the data?

- How does this relate to social and emotional competencies?

Attuning to the Individuals on Your SEL Team

This is important because these are the central people doing the work with you. You want to make sure you understand them. Attunement describes how reactive you are to another's emotional needs and moods. Someone who is well attuned will respond with appropriate language and behaviors based on another person's emotional state. This nonverbal communication is more reliable than verbal communication especially if there is inconsistency in what you are saying and what your nonverbals are saying. Thinking through some of these ways to respond is a great first start in attuning to others. When in doubt we trust the nonverbal message over the verbal message. The nonverbal is seen as being more trustworthy because it demonstrates the intention of the sender and reflects their emotional reactions while words can be more easily manipulated. In a 2017 study, researchers found a correlation between teachers' verbal and nonverbal communication skills and students' learning and motivation. This is another reason that we should focus on aligning our verbal and nonverbal behavior (Bambaeeroo & Shokrpour, 2017).

TASK: Individual meetings with team members

The SEL coach may want to have additional meetings with each team member individually to discuss:

- How are you feeling being a part of this team?

- Do you feel that your voice matters with this group? Do you feel you are heard?

- What is one thing that you believe would help you to feel more connected to this group and the work that you are doing?

- What are the SEL team's strengths? Weaknesses?

- Is time used well?

- What is your favorite thing? Least favorite thing?

PHASE 4: SEL TEAM ROLE TASKS

Check-In

You will need to do periodic check-ins with administrators and school leaders. This information will be important for the further growth and development of your SEL team. In phase 4, how will the team continue moving the work forward? Do they evolve to something else?

- What is an area in which you feel you SEL team is making good progress?

- What areas in SEL would you like to focus on until the end of the school year?

- What area of focus would you like your SEL coach to practice between now and the end of the school year?

RANDI PETERSON

Social Emotional Learning Curriculum Developer

Washington

Interview:

1. *What did you find was most effective about the program or practice?*

   *I found that it was critical to do this work **with** teachers and families (not to them or for them). Building adult SEL was critical in the process. We cannot ask teachers to teach SEL overnight (they may not have experienced a formal Tier 1 curriculum when they were students). SEL is complicated because we are required to simultaneously build adult skills and confidence and teach students.*

2. *What did you find did **not** work during the program implementation?*

   Adopting a curriculum and telling teachers to teach it doesn't work— adult buy-in is often the biggest barrier to SEL. It is critical to start with adults first.

3. *What is the best way to increase schoolwide implementation of social emotional learning in your experience?*

   The best way to increase schoolwide implementation is to leverage teacher leaders. I have teacher champions (Student Well-Being Leads) who earn a leadership stipend each year. It always helps when you pay and feed staff. Getting staff involved from the beginning is key. Sharing success stories showcasing actual district staff (not some school in another district or state) really helps with implementation. It is also critical to include families in the process as partners in the rollout and home connection to what is happening at school. I find that the vast majority of parents want to support the SEL of their child but sometimes lack the skills and strategies. We need to build the skills, strategies, and competence of families as well—they are key stakeholders in this work.

4. Were there any key turning points during implementation?

Identifying (and compensating) Student Well-Being Leads in each building (18 in all) was the most impactful thing that I did. It became an SEL PLC and then collaboration supported and impacted all 18 of our buildings positively with the implementation and sustainability of SEL. Having Student Well-Being Leads share the innovative things that they were doing to support implementation and to keep it a focus among other initiatives in their building with one another was invaluable.

5. What were the key relationships that mattered most? What were the key sources of support or resistance you encountered?

It was key to have all those who see themselves leading the work in the building working in collaboration—instructional coaches, counselors, and Student Well-Being Leads. Such buildings are the most successful when building leaders own and support the work.

6. What was most difficult or challenging? What did you do to deal with these challenges?

The most challenging part of leading this work for me was when a group in our community came forward to challenge the work we were doing. There was a large constituent group that opposed mindfulness and made this work political. It was hard.

7. What was most rewarding?

The most rewarding piece is being out in buildings doing learning walks and talking with students and seeing evidence of our SEL efforts. It's heartwarming to hear the students use key phrases from our curriculum and to see them put it into practice in authentic settings.

8. What are the lessons you would pass on for other people in your role?

Find support. Create a PLC within your district and in your region. It's critical to have a peer group to support your work. Also, it is very encouraging to have others to celebrate your successes with and to problem solve with when needed.

9. *If you could do this implementation over again, would you do anything differently? Why, and what would you do?*

   Proactively get students involved. I also highly recommend getting students involved and including student voice where you can. Our students have some incredible insights and they can be invaluable in the process.

10. *Do you view your contributions as successful? In what ways? What specifically was accomplished?*

    Working in collaboration with teams of counselors, instruction coaches, and leads has been invaluable. Participating in SEL learning walks has helped to strengthen implementation and SEL in general. It's amazing how much we can learn when we get out of our buildings and see what others are doing.

11. *When you think of the future of Social Emotional Learning in your system or your work, what gives you a sense of hope? What makes you concerned or worried?*

    I have hope because SEL is a key component in our district strategic plan. Given that we have districtwide goals related to our strategic plan hold us accountable to the School Board. I am a little concerned that some folks are just waiting for this ship to sail. Those who haven't been brought into SEL at this point just seem to be waiting for it to go away and for another initiative to take over.

CHAPTER 6

....

ADVANCE YOUR PRACTICE

Data Support

PHASE 1: DATA SUPPORT ROLE TASKS

SEL coaches may need to both gather data and train teachers on how to use it to improve their practices. This part of the coaching role is the most effective and least trained. It will be important for the coach to get data for teachers and help train teachers on how to help with collection and analysis. Working with data, the SEL coach must both use what they have and discover what they need. The first step is to understand and gather the data that is already out there and available. Begin with the district webpage, school webpage, state data, and local sources of data collected by the school. Once you understand the data that currently exists, the SEL coach will have to determine the best way to actively understand their system. This includes things like establishing a data system to monitor progress and aid in decision-making, including the teacher's surveys, questionnaires, needs assessments, universal screeners, skill assessments, and a tiered fidelity inventory.

In a phased implementation, the data would be focused on previously collected data, including an examination of the discipline, attendance, and surveys (Healthy Youth Survey, panorama, beliefs, exit survey, etc.) and observations, previous implementation, staff vote, student data, universal screener, and needs assessment, if applicable. Not every school will have the access to all this data. Some states don't make the Healthy Youth Survey mandatory, and others don't do school climate assessments. The SEL coach will take the lead in discovering the data that is already available to begin to create a picture of the school from a 10,000-foot vantage. In phase 2, you may decide to actively implement some additional data tracking system. In phase 3, you will use the data collected to identify how current interventions are working, if there is a need for change, and the effects of interventions. The SEL can collect, analyze, and disseminate data. The team and principal can make decisions based on the data collected. This data will be invaluable in driving decision-making and evaluating outcomes. But we must recognize that the adoption, collection, and dissemination will all be dependent on the school and the outcomes being evaluated by the SEL teams and within consultation with teachers and other educational stakeholders.

Administrators find the data collector role to be most effective when they provide gentle accountability for the system, where SEL coaches are sharing data from their specific school, where it can be collected and reviewed in-house. The SEL coach is essential in building a decision-making process for building and bringing specific data to central leadership as needed.

Qualitative vs. Quantitative Data

Qualitative evaluations include three kinds of data collection that include in-depth, open-ended interviews, direct observation, and written documents (Patton, 2003). It is very powerful in combination with quantitative (numerical) data. Interviews about educators' experiences, perceptions, opinions, feelings, and knowledge are helpful to understand their specific experiences. But in combination with other interviews, they can provide a look at patterns and themes that are repeated with these unique experiences. Observations include descriptions of activities, behaviors, actions, and conversations. The data comes in the form of field notes or detailed descriptions (Patton, 2003) and documents, which are materials from records, emails, notes, reports, or written responses to open-ended surveys. One example of how qualitative and quantitative information can be gathered and interpreted is through a questionnaire. The questionnaire can ask questions that can be assigned a value, as in a Likert score rating 1–5. It can also contain open-ended questions.

The way to think about the types of data is through a timeline structured in order of how to collect it: historical, culture/climate, screener (formal/informal), post-intervention, progress monitoring, and finally outcome data.

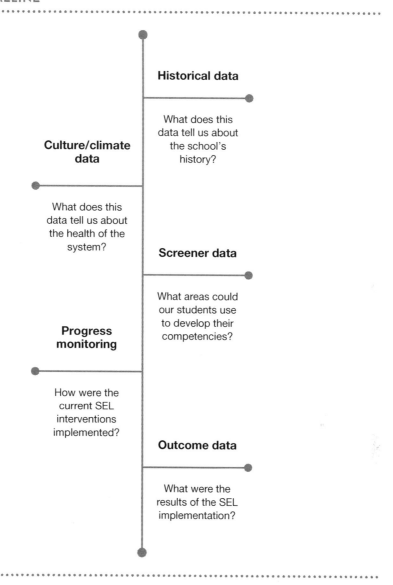

Historical data

What does this data tell us about the school's history?

Culture/climate data

What does this data tell us about the health of the system?

Screener data

What areas could our students use to develop their competencies?

Progress monitoring

How were the current SEL interventions implemented?

Outcome data

What were the results of the SEL implementation?

Historical Data: Understand Historical Data by Creating a School Snapshot

The historical data gives us a picture of the school's history and why some decisions were made. The SEL coach should begin to understand the context of their school. Creating a "school snapshot" is the data that currently exists and is a one-stop place for all your information. Anything that will help us construct a narrative that tells us where you started is valuable. This includes the need for SEL and an SEL coach.

- How was the position of SEL coach funded?

- What has SEL looked like in the school in the past?

- Who are the proponents of SEL in your school?

- What is the role of higher-level administration (superintendent, school board, etc.)?

- What need is SEL meant to help with?

- What data was used to determine the need?

Climate and Culture Data

SEL coaches should consider using a Climate and Culture Observation tool that provides indicators of a positive and supportive learning environment required for students to engage in academically rigorous instruction and develop appropriate social and emotional skills. The tool is not an exhaustive list of indicators but does provide specific, concrete look-fors while allowing the observer to capture additional information not reflected in the observation tool. Some of the elements in this tool include identifying practices that gauge collaboration, engagement, and evidence of student–teacher relationships. A classroom assessment tool can provide information about the overall classroom environment, how teachers relate to and build relationships with students, and the quality of the learning environment (Leff et al., 2011). The behaviors that can be coded in this type of observation can include noncompliance and disruptive behavior, teacher reprimand, teacher praise, students in class demonstrating interest and enthusiasm, and the students focusing and being on task. This information can be useful in determining if specific interventions are useful in ameliorating issues in the school setting (Leff et al., 2011).

TASK: Using culture/climate assessments to create a social and emotional competence data set

The SEL coach may have to create a self-report data set that focuses specifically on topics related to social and emotional competencies. The data set will include question, topic/construct, grade/age, score range, etc.

Example:

QUESTION	TOPIC	GRADE	SOURCE	DISTRICT RESULTS
I like working with a partner or small groups in my classes.	Classroom environment	6	Needs assessment	89%
My teacher asks for my opinions in school.	Classroom environment	6	Needs assessment	61%
I feel safe at school.	School climate	6	Climate assessment	96%
My classmates are respectful.	School climate	6	Climate assessment	48%
I help others at school when they need it.	School climate	6	Climate assessment	91%
My teacher teaches us about behavior expectations in class.	Communication skills	6	Student rating	78%
My teacher tells me when I am doing a good job.	Communication skills	6	Student rating	82%

As I mentioned in *Leading for Change Through Whole School Social Emotional Learning*, I have seen when schools collect large data sets without having decision rules, and they are at a loss for what to do with the data (Rogers, 2019). For large data sets, it is important to understand the decision rules for services. This is especially true when working in a tiered system. At the universal level, all students will receive services. But the services can be tailored to the specifics of the large data sets. If we determine that students are "at risk," we must understand what that means and what your large data set can and cannot tell you. Before you begin, learn how your school or district makes decision rules. How are schools receiving services and how do students qualify for additional supports? Are your decision rules documented? What is the cut score for students who get the additional interventions? SEL coaches who understand how students have historically received services at each tiered intervention level will help you use the data you collect more efficiently (Rogers, 2019).

PHASE 2: DATA SUPPORT ROLE TASKS

Create SMART Goals

Action planning uses data to drive decisions included in the beginning of the plan. It guides what the teams do. Therefore, it is important to include this type of action planning for each step of the intervention. It creates a sense of responsibility and accountability for the team members. But remember to set concrete, short-term goals or SMART (specific, measurable, attainable,

GOALS	QUALITIES	WHAT DOES IT LOOK LIKE IN SEL IMPLEMENTATION?	WHAT IS THE ACTION PLAN?
Specific	Who, what, when, where, how, why?		
Measurable	What metric can you use to measure use or attainment?		
Attainable	Are the goals realistic?		
Relevant	Connected closely to the objective		
Timely	What is a completion date that holds it accountable?		

relevant, timely) goals to keep the pace of the intervention in a meaningful way.

Create "In-the-Moment" Data Collection Sources (Informal Data)

In some of the schools I have worked in, I recommend "guerilla" data collection practices. These are tactics in which a small group uses irregular methods to understand the larger group. These brief hit-and-run methods do not give you the large amounts of data that a screener, needs assessment or survey may give. But it will help you understand the system a little better with only minor costs in time and energy (Rogers, 2019). One of the strategies that I recommend is the morning check-in/goal setting. Every morning the students answer three multiple-choice or long-form questions. These questions could cover any topics, three quick questions about their academic, class, and personal goals; all goals align with the specific self-management, relationship skills, and responsible decision-making skills that we are hoping to teach them. With the Google Form, you can see the class goals as a whole and individual student goals. And educators can change the goals when students have received instruction and seem to grasp concepts that you are focused on.

Use a Google Form like the one pictured here to ask developmentally appropriate check-in questions that align with Social Emotional Learning.

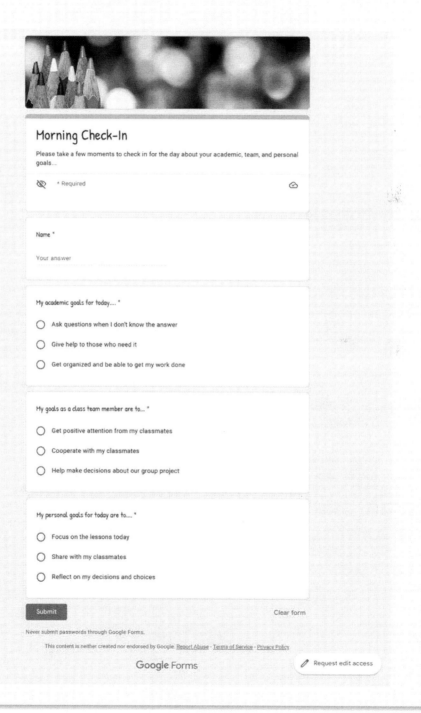

When Choosing an Assessment:
Universal Screener (Formal Data)

There are things to consider prior to using a universal screener. What is the cut-off score for next-level interventions? Individual vs. group score? You will also need to consider some of the more technical aspects when choosing a universal screener for your school: appropriateness for the intended use, technical adequacy, usability, determination of the optimal informant, and treatment validity (Cook et al., 2010). There are other data points that need to be considered in conjunction with the results of a universal screener to give us a more complete picture of the student and their needs for additional services. Other factors in the decision-making process are the number of discipline referrals, the number of absences, changes in behavior, and any known change in the student's home situation.

Prior to using a universal screener, schools will want to consider resource mapping. This is to help determine what is available at your school. If we are to recommend tiered interventions, it is beneficial to see what you can provide for students who need additional resources. The process of resource mapping is a good way to understand some of the gaps as well.

The universal screener will require a problem-solving process for universal SEL implementation. You can use the data collected from a universal screener to help with teaching school or classroomwide competencies as well as interventions for individuals and small groups. You may find a competency need based on an increased level of a particular behavior (at-risk internalizing or at-risk externalizing). You see from the data that there are common groups with specific needs. For example, there is an increase in disruptive behavior amongst second-grade girls. You can use a problem-solving plan and after you determine the optimal strategies. You will need to go back to the data and find out. Did the intervention mediate the issue?

A few students will need to move on to Tier 2 interventions. This is based on the cutoff score for individual students (internalizing, externalizing, or both) who are identified as needing more intensive interventions. There will be things to consider prior to recommending specific students to Tier 2 interventions. This includes their current competency development, family involvement, grades, test scores, and if they also need academic interventions. You will also want to consider their interpersonal skills and what you can provide them in Tier 2. This can include self-management/social skills, a recognition system for social skills, small group (e.g., grief, friendship issues), or counseling (e.g., trauma). If possible, involve the student in the selection of interventions that will match their perceived needs as well. We want to do what works for the student in the best way that we can.

Resource mapping: What is available at your school—universal, targeted, and intensive interventions—that can connect your students needs from a universal screener?

- SEL curriculum

- Everyday SEL practices

- Active skill building

- Academic integration with SEL

- Adult mentoring

- Social and life skills training

- Reward matching for a specific kid

- Increased monitoring

- Parent collaboration/support/training

- Outside agency services

- Community service

- Teaching "thinking skills"

- Staff review of classroom management

- Promote prosocial behavior through school involvement progress

- Group counseling

- Other

PHASE 3: DATA SUPPORT ROLE TASKS

Problem-Solving Action Plan

It is recommended to use a problem-solving process to determine the direction of your universal SEL efforts. This is a way to determine your focus based on your specific needs. Data collection and analysis drive the next steps in our SEL work. We use data to drive our decisions systemically and with individual students and scenarios. Looking at systemic data may involve a multistep process that looks at different parts of the problem and tries to solve for all the parts. There are many benefits to using this type of problem-solving process during your SEL implementation. This information can be collected to see if there are specific problems that you are seeing schoolwide, to design trainings for specific SEL strategies that are regularly used, and/or to determine which curriculum to purchase based on student SEL competency needs. One recommended problem-solving method looks at the following (Rathvon, 2008):

- Stage 1: Problem definition
  - Step 1: Defining the issue
  - Step 2: Clarifying the problem
  - Step 3: Obtaining baseline data
- Stage 2: Problem analysis
  - Step 4: Conducting an ecological analysis of the problem
  - Step 5: Exploring intervention strategies
  - Step 6: Selecting interventions
  - Step 7: Developing the intervention plan
- Stage 3: Plan implementation
  - Step 8: Implementing the intervention plan
- Stage 4: Plan evaluation
  - Step 9: Evaluating intervention plan effectiveness
  - Step 10: Continued problem-solving, plan revision, and possible referral

This form can be used in your system to help build a process for universal problem-solving.

Problem-Solving Process: Universal SEL

Stage 1

Name/s:_____

Class/Grade/Team: _____

Date:_____

Instructions: Fill out this sheet with as much detail as possible.

What issues are you seeing in your class or school?

_____

_____

_____

_____

How many students does it involve? And how long has it been going on?

_____

_____

_____

_____

What do you think the issue is? What is their behavior communicating? Is there a skill deficiency?

_____

_____

_____

_____

(Continued)

(Continued)

What have you tried before? What worked and did not work about that strategy?

_____

_____

_____

_____

What data have you collected about the issue? Examples: observation, discussion, climate survey, universal screener, student report, survey, etc.

_____

_____

_____

_____

What factors could be contributing to the problem? Peers? Classroom? Curriculum? Changes in school or home environment?

_____

_____

_____

_____

FOR SEL COACH USE ONLY:

Date received: _____

Meeting for Stage 2 set: Time _____/Date_____

Problem-Solving Process: Universal SEL

Stage 2

Name/s: _____

Class/Grade/Team: _____

Date: _____

Instructions: SEL coach will read Stage 1 information, process the available data, and prepare a few intervention strategies as solutions to explore with the teacher or team.

What does the data suggest as the potential skills that could be worked on to remediate the issue?

_____

_____

_____

Recommended intervention strategies to explore (list and describe)

1. _____

_____

2. _____

_____

3. _____

_____

Intervention selected and why?

_____

_____

_____

_____

FOR SEL COACH USE ONLY:

Date received: _____

Meeting for Stage 3 set: Time _____ /Date _____

(Continued)

(Continued)

Problem-Solving Process: Universal SEL

Stage 3

Name/s:_____

Class/Grade/Team: _____

Date: _____

Instructions: SEL coach will read Stage 2 information, process the available data, and prepare a few intervention strategies as solutions to explore with the teacher or team.

The plan

Goal: What will it look like when there is no longer an issue?

_____

_____

Plan for teaching the intervention:

_____

_____

Plan to practice the competency:

_____

_____

Plan for modeling the competency:

_____

_____

Plan for supporting the competency:

_____

_____

Stage 3: Implementation Check-In

Date 1:_____ Date 2: _____

Date 3: _____

FOR SEL COACH USE ONLY:

Meeting for Stage 4 set: Time _____/Date _____

Problem-Solving Process: Universal SEL

Stage 4

Name/s:_____

Class/Grade/Team: _____

Date:_____

Instructions: SEL coach will review previous stages and check-in information, process the available data, and prepare to meet with the teacher or team.

Did we reach the goal as set in Stage 2? What improvements were made? What barriers still exist?

_____

_____

_____

_____

Options for next steps:

Looking at the data, our next step is to:

☐ Maintain existing supports

☐ Use a different universal strategy

☐ Stop existing supports

☐ Referral to Tier 2 team or Tier 3 (SPED referral)

Plan for next step:
FOR SEL COACH USE ONLY:
Date received: _____
Next step: _____ Maintain _____ Different Universal _____
Stop _____ Refer to higher tier team

Progress Monitoring With a Tiered Fidelity Inventory

Fidelity of implementation means common understanding and consistency in practices across all stakeholders. The main purpose of this instrument is to help school teams improve their efficacy to better understand your system and its needs. The purpose is not to be an instrument to exert negative pressure on individuals if they have not made a certain benchmark in a specific time. The hope is to understand more about your system and create a record to reflect on things that worked and did not work over time.

In my work, I recommend a tiered fidelity inventory to be used as a progress-monitoring instrument. The group self-assessment is meant to guide practices of the implementation process by each phase. Stakeholders will be able to look at the progress by each subgroup. This will help build action plans to focus on implementation efforts. The data can include qualitative, quantitative, and historical data. I use the metaphor that we are building a mosaic and with each piece of data, we are understanding more about the school, students, and educators who work within the school year after year. The tiered fidelity inventory is one of those pieces.

The SEL coach needs to conduct assessments of students and/or their learning environment for program supports as necessary. This may be done through classroom observations and drop-bys. The coach can record the results of those meetings and any progress that has been made as part of the tiered fidelity inventory.

TASK: Create or adopt a tiered fidelity inventory

	PHASE 1	DATA SOURCES	SCORING CRITERIA	SCORE
Vision and goals	Establish vision and goals	• Documents • Meeting notes • Graphics • Goals communicated on the school website	☐ District vision ☐ School vision ☐ District goals ☐ School goals	___/4
SEL teams	Establish SEL teams	• List of team members • Team norms • Team roles • Agendas • Notes • Action plan • Team trainings	☐ Not formed a team (0 points) ☐ Each feature (1 point)	___/6

	PHASE 1	DATA SOURCES	SCORING CRITERIA	SCORE
Training educational stakeholders across the system	Determine needs for systemwide training	• Action plan for PD • PD for teachers • PD for administrators • Training for universal teams • PD for paraprofessionals	☐ No process for teaching educational stakeholders in place (0 points) ☐ The professional development and orientation process is informal (1 point) ☐ A written process is used to teach all relevant staff in SEL foundational practices (1 point for each training)	____ total points
Data collection system	Review current data for social, emotional, and behavioral competencies	• Healthy Youth Survey data • School climate data • Exit survey data • School survey data • Behavior data • Discipline data • Crisis/counseling • Social and emotional competencies	☐ No process/ protocol exists (0 points) ☐ Data is reviewed but not used (1 point) ☐ Data reviewed and used for decision-making (3 points) ☐ Regular meetings to review data (5 points) ☐ An action plan is developed to enhance or modify universal supports based on data (10 points)	____ total points
Tiered practices	Identify universal interventions currently used	• Examples of relationship-building strategies used in your school • Examples of engagement strategies used in your school • Use of everyday SEL practices	☐ Developed relationship building skills across the school (10 points) ☐ Developed engagement building skills across the school (10 points)	____ total points

(Continued)

(Continued)

	PHASE 1	DATA SOURCES	SCORING CRITERIA	SCORE
		• Evidence of Social Emotional Learning curriculum • Use of active skill building • Plans for academic inclusion • Examples of adult SEL	☐ Developed everyday SEL practices across the school (10 points) ☐ Selected a curriculum or curriculums (5 points) ☐ Plan for use of SEL curriculum (10 points) ☐ Developed active skills for social and emotional competencies (10 points) ☐ Developed plans for academic inclusion (10 points) ☐ Developed programming for Adult SEL (10 points)	＿＿ total points
Share progress and outcomes	Create Year 1 report	• Parent/family meeting agendas • PowerPoints • Handouts • Workshop materials • Newsletters • Emails • School websites • Brochures • Year 1 report	☐ No communications were sent out to the school community (0 points) ☐ Some documentation of communication but not from all types of stakeholders (1 point) ☐ Documentation of communication exists that students, families, and community members have access to (2 points) ☐ Year 1 report created and disseminated to educational stakeholders (5 points)	＿＿ total points
				Total points = ＿＿

PHASE 4: DATA SUPPORT ROLE TASKS

Learning More About Strategies
Used by Individual Teachers

This is a good and potentially anonymous way to find out what strategies are being used to build relationships with students. After the data has been coded and tallied, you can use it for various purposes.

TASK: How to code your current strategies

For example, what strategy is represented most/least? Do we see more specific strategies being used by specific grade levels? If we see a lot of a specific type of strategy, can we use it to build upon to add another social emotional competency?

Referring to the example that follows (see p. 112):

1. Ask teachers to write down the strategies that they currently use to build relationships with students. Label each school at the top of the worksheet.

2. Read each strategy. See if any statement falls under one of our current strategies for Self-Awareness (SA), Social Awareness (SOA), Relationship Skills (RS), Self-Management (SM), Responsible Decision-Making (RDM), and Academic (ACA), on the list. Write a tally mark on the total section of the worksheet.

3. List strategies such as academic interventions in another box.

4. For each strategy that does not seem to fit with any of the competencies and is not considered an academic strategy, mark them in the "?" column.

5. Total tally marks in each column and circle them in the "Totals" boxes.

BASIC HIGH SCHOOL TOTAL RESPONDENTS: 74	SA	SOA	RS	SM	RDM	ACA	?
Greeted them each day							
Made a difference to talk to them one-on-one and told them I am concerned and offered help							
Talked with them after class to have check-ins to start the conversation							
Let them know I care							
Provided resources for kids							
Tried to build a relationship: less curriculum to cover to spend more time with my kids							
Demonstrated patience, attempted to build relationships, built kids up, got to know their friends							
Listened to them							
Set aside 5 minutes a day to chat, laugh, etc. Worked on close-proximity seating							
Spent one-on-one time, chatting, and helping them through assignments							
Positive classroom atmosphere. Open door—was able to work/relax in the classroom. Helped with schoolwork. Listened. Tried to understand/relate							
Took time to get to know them and let them know I care. Encouraged and praised small and large successes. Helped foster a strong, positive self-concept							
Shred feedback on behavior with positive rewards. Taught social skills that helped them with peer relationships. Offered unconditional support but held them accountable							
TOTALS:							

Understanding Evaluation Outcomes

One way to evaluate your outcomes is to look at outcomes that have been proven through previous studies. Some of the evaluation outcomes listed in the graphic are from the seminal meta-analysis in 2011. These are ways that SEL has been demonstrated to improve outcomes. Here are some ideas for how to understand the direct and indirect assessments of gains to the system.

The first is to understand if there has been improved academic performance. That can be measured through grades, test scores, summative assessments, and the like. The second is increased positive social behavior. It can be measured through attendance, school climate measures, and determining if the students have learned to work well with others, if there are reports of positive peer relations, or if there is evidence of conflict resolution. To measure if there are reduced conduct problems, SEL coaches can use the quantity of referrals, suspensions, retentions, and aggressive and disruptive behavior. To measure reduced emotional distress, the SEL coach can use the data collected on rates of students who ask for or receive counseling, crisis, depressive symptoms, anxiety, social withdrawal, and more.

Implementation of SEL classroom approaches can be measured as well. This would include an understanding of who is teaching and when explicit instruction of SEL is happening in your building. Is there a focus on teaching skills that can be broadly applied to a variety of situations such as making friends, working cooperatively with others, coping with stress, and resolving interpersonal conflicts? Is there a practice or process for integration of SEL with academic curriculum areas? These are lessons with academic content while also developing social emotional competencies. Teacher instructional practices focus on instructional processes, pedagogies, and management approaches to promote a positive classroom climate and practices that support positive relationships among teachers and students and foster conditions for learning (e.g., authentic praise or involving students in decision-making). Finally, the SEL coach can measure the resources of time that are dedicated to supporting practice within the school and classroom. Does administration provide opportunities to practice social and emotional skills? This includes consistent opportunities for practice of skills both within classroom lessons and beyond lessons in daily situations. Often, this must be an explicit expectation set and supported by the administration to happen.

There are schoolwide approaches that are contexts that promote and reinforce SEL. These things can include places beyond the classroom SEL program and schoolwide practices that promote collaboration among classrooms, grade levels, and so on. It can include evaluation of family programming and outreach such as homework for family, workshops, and activities. You may even consider measuring community impact and the interactive involvement of students and community members.

The evaluation outcomes can include the methods that you choose to use as assessment tools. How do you monitor implementation? It can include how you use a self-report (teachers, administration, school stakeholders), surveys, and observations. Evaluation outcomes can be measured by student behavior through baseline assessments like screeners and your overall school data collection.

These methods can be invaluable in demonstrating the work that the SEL coach, the SEL team, and the educational stakeholders have done to help students and adults develop social and emotional competencies that will help them.

TASK: Develop an evaluation document

SCHOOL OUTCOMES AND IMPLICATIONS OF CHANGE

SCHOOL OUTCOMES	HISTORICAL DATA	CURRENT FINDINGS	IMPLICATIONS OF CHANGE
Academic performance			
Social behavior			
Conduct problems			
Emotional distress			
Engagement			
Safety			
Environment			

STACEY KNIGHT

Social Emotional Coach

Wisconsin

Interview:

1. *Can you tell me a few things that worked in your SEL implementation? Or a few things that did not work, that you don't recommend?*

   What has been important is incorporating the perspective of other people, the teachers, and the building administrators. It is not that it has necessarily been challenging, and it is listening to all perspectives and considering how to implement and incorporate those ideas into universal/grade level practices. I have to understand from the teachers' perspective the integration and how to support them and students universally with this work. They know best how to incorporate SEL within daily work and schedules, thereby, considering how I support integration of their thoughts and perspectives into universal SEL structures and lessons.

2. *How did you manage getting everyone's perspectives for the work?*

   I reviewed and explained with teachers possible SEL material options, getting their feedback. This allowed me to then take that information back to help a team pick the materials being implemented. As an SEL coach, I think it's really important that I started by co-planning with teachers the SEL lessons. I strongly feel an important early step is to start with co-planning in the building to support the staff. This helps provide the why and the how of SEL relating to new concepts teaching and concepts/structures already in place. As a facilitator, co-planning with grade-level teams allows me to support vertically and horizontally, providing insight/context of the concepts throughout the building.

3. *When you were doing the co-planning, did it make sense to you to select volunteers, or did you have any pushback in this process?*

   I have co-planned with all teachers, then offered to co-teach. I support lesson delivery by coaching lesson integration, order, and common language. I co-teach with those teachers who initiate and want the support. I believe one part of SEL coaching and co-teaching that is a difficult but important part is explaining I'm there to support and work with them and not judge them. Together we're delivering SEL lessons and supporting the students. I have begun the next step with staff getting a little bit deeper in the coaching process by reviewing previous steps and providing feedback.

4. How long did it take for you to get to coaching or co-teaching?

   Coaching SEL within a universal system, I started about five to seven years ago. The key is to go slow in the process. Going slow allows for a better understanding of the why, structures, and consistent implementation. I feel it helps build trust through the process, which is really important between all parties. The foundation of trust allows two-way communication and receptivity to feedback.

5. How have you been able to sustain over seven years of doing this?

   It has changed over time. I have gone from meeting with staff at the beginning discussing thoughts, logistics, and structures. Next, collaborating with grade-level teams on a monthly basis to lesson-plan and support implementation. As well as, from co-planning stand-alone SEL lessons to coaching incorporation of SEL concepts into academic lessons. I have been fortunate that others I have worked with have seen SEL as important as academics. I have had time to work with staff due to being a priority, as well as the other areas. I think now as other things become a priority and we are getting further on in the process, some of that time has been diminished. It is still important to meet with the teachers and staff on a regular basis. As a facilitator/coach without providing time to co-plan, co-teach, observe, provide feedback, and check in on an ongoing basis, I feel SEL integration can decrease due to other demands/priorities.

6. What data do you use for universal practices of SEL?

   Prior to current environmental circumstances, I was seeing a decrease in the number of students who needed group support in a Tier 2 intervention. This decrease was not completely scientific. I noticed a decrease in intervention group numbers, office discipline referral (ODR) data, and a decrease in teacher submissions requesting student SEL support. Given all those pieces of information, intervention numbers were much lower than they had been previously. I believe one of the factors was due to teaching and supporting universal implementation within the building, providing students with concepts and strategies for social emotional regulation and interactions.

7. *When you think of the future of Social Emotional Learning in your system or your work, what gives you a sense of hope? What makes you concerned or worried?*

Most rewarding, I have observed staff and students utilizing the common language/concepts of the universal SEL skills to express and manage their thoughts/feelings and during interactions with each other. This allows for a better understanding and response with each other. Thinking of the future, I hope the continuation of SEL common language, concepts, and strategies are taught/reinforced for students' expected responses to all situations. Not only is student and staff knowledge of common language important, but I've also had parents reach out seeking understanding of the common language and strategies being taught to incorporate within the home setting as well. It is really important to make home/school connections. I've responded by sharing with parents the specific common language and strategies students are learning. For the future, I am continuing to build home/school connections and sharing SEL concepts and strategies with them from a universal level. I believe we are not only building these SEL skills from a school perspective, but we are also building skills that can be transferred to the home and community.

A concern within SEL implementation I have is how to keep prioritizing this work. Necessarily, focuses continue to change, but how will buildings continue to prioritize this work for the future?

Given this work takes time to fully implement and outcomes are sometimes not immediately evident, allow yourself to have the mindset that this is OK while gathering evidence to show progress. I have observed prioritizing SEL to support individual student social emotional well-being and interactions. Hopefully down the road, all will see those outcomes universally.

CHAPTER 7

....

ADVANCE YOUR PRACTICE

Professional Development

As an SEL coach, your role will likely include training groups of individuals for professional development. This is often where the educational stakeholders will be introduced to systemwide practices of SEL. You will need to continue to work to gain clarity of role and SEL implementation. Give them updates on the SEL implementation work so far. The PD should contain expectations and logistics with schoolwide practices. And the SEL coach will be wise to be sensitive to overwhelming staff with new information.

It may be helpful to think about how to organize your thinking about professional development: Consider some of the things that you "must" think about prior to the session and ideas you may have. Next, plan what to do while training for the intervention and look-fors. And after, describe what you discovered about how it went and what are others' takeaways. And finally, conclude what was the efficacy of the PD.

An appropriate progression of PD for schools new to SEL is first to provide training about what SEL is and is not and why it is something that your school will want to focus on. Initially, it will be an introduction of the concepts, theories, and impact of SEL to get all the educational stakeholders with a baseline understanding. Then PD can move on to any data collection that has been done to guide the focus of the implementation. Staff would be instructed on how to use this data to choose interventions that will help with skill acquisition. After that, all professional development will follow the implementation needs in an iterative process. The SEL coach will learn more about what is working and not working. And they will discuss with staff some of the celebrations and action plans based on their new discoveries.

The support and promotion of SEL schoolwide directly affect the educators' comfort in regular implementation of curricula, everyday practices, and active learning in the classroom of teachers (Collie et al., 2012). As a result of professional development, we should see teachers using data about social and emotional competencies, school culture, and the like to drive the decisions that are made both in individual classrooms and systemwide. Students will take an active part in their own learning in both academic and social emotional domains. And there will be a variety of interventions implemented sustainably and with fidelity throughout the system to meet the needs of students and adults.

The following factors affect the SEL implementation process for teachers: the perceived need for innovation (the extent to which the proposed innovation is relevant to local needs); perceived benefits of innovation (the extent to which the innovation will achieve benefits desired at the local level); self-efficacy (the extent to which providers feel they are or will be able to do what is expected); and skill proficiency (possession of the skills necessary for implementation) (Durlak & DuPre, 2008). The SEL coach will need to focus specifically on these things during PD. And teachers will require technical assistance: the combination of resources offered to providers once implementation begins, and may include retraining in certain skills, training of new staff, emotional support, and mechanisms to promote local problem-solving efforts (Durlak & DuPre, 2008).

PHASE 1: PROFESSIONAL DEVELOPMENT ROLE TASKS

Universal Social Emotional Learning

Many educational systems use MTSS (multitiered systems of support) or MLSS (multilayered systems of support) to structure their interventions. It is a data-driven, problem-solving framework designed to improve the outcomes of all students. It is important to use evidence-based practices in this work to provide interventions that will help all students thrive in the school environment. Even if your school or district has not adopted this specific system of support, it will be helpful for you to integrate its use in the way that you look at the system.

MTSS provides the scaffolding to meet individual students' academic, social, emotional, and behavioral needs. Tier 1 strategies are for ALL students. This includes students who may qualify for additional levels of support. Tier 1 supports are designed to benefit all students in a manner that is proactive and preventative. It can help to build a solid foundation to build upon, so all students are receiving a baseline education in social and emotional competencies. Some examples of universal or universal interventions can include effective academic support, social emotional learning curriculum and active practices, schoolwide expectations, equity, and classroom management. Tier 2 Social Emotional Learning can be used to complement the universal strategies. Often, these students are determined by a universal screener or team recommendation. This extra support allows students to practice these skills in smaller, more tailored environments. Examples include small groups to teach self-regulation, increased academic support, and check-in and check-out procedures. Tier 3 in social and emotional education is for more intensive interventions to learn and practice social and emotional skills. They often include more intensive supports like adult mentors, parent/guardian training, or wraparound services from outside school providers that collaborate with the school-based staff. In your system, the connections need to be multidimensional where students are receiving support in universal, regardless of whether they qualify for services in Tier 2 or Tier 3.

The purpose of tiered interventions is to ensure equity of service where all students have access to obtaining these crucial skills and meet the needs of all students. SEL coaches will often find themselves in situations where a teacher will ask them to observe one student. Specifically, there are students who are particularly struggling and who teachers feel need additional help. Those observations often result in the realization that the teacher does not have any proactive whole class strategies in place to help all their students. Then the coach is put in a difficult place where they must advocate for universal SEL interventions when the teacher just wants help with this one child "and then everything would be okay." It will require a strategy to be able to shift the conversation and ways of thinking. This can require working on beliefs and practices that have been honed over time. The teacher may think that they don't have the time and effort to change the things that work for all kids. Therefore, it is important at a systems level to make sure that everyone understands the benefits of emphasizing strategies that enhance the functioning of the entire class rather than just a target student (Rathvon, 2008), Universal strategies are more efficient in time and labor. Using the same strategy for all kids can be more efficient. It helps to avoid singling students and can avoid the fairness issue for students who see that some kids receive more (resources, time, etc.) than some other kids. When teaching all students, they can reinforce the use of the skill as a norm for the whole classroom. And there can be a positive impact on the function of all students in the class (Rathvon, 2008).

Social Emotional Learning takes a prevention science perspective (Herman et al., 2020). And prevention is universal; it conceptualizes problems in terms of risk and protective factors. Protective factors are conditions or attributes in individuals that increase their well-being. Some examples of protective factors are social skills, emotional control, and interactions with prosocial peers. All these things are taught and practiced as part of SEL. Protective factors also help to reduce risk factors that make students more susceptible to bullying, impulsiveness, and friendships who exhibit problematic behaviors. Prevention science perspectives are skills focused.

1. Who are universal SEL strategies for?

   Answer: All students, all staff. When you work with staff, it is important to start where their beliefs are.

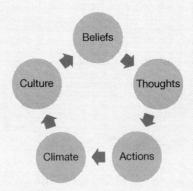

Belief: Teachers have a powerful role in students' lives and how they see themselves.

Thoughts: I can affect students' lives in a positive way.

Actions: I make a point to tell students when I recognize their talent and abilities.

Climate: Teachers feel positive about their relationships with students.

Culture: Teachers here regularly practice social emotional skills with their students.

Social Emotional Learning is beneficial to the individuals who adopt the skills and strategies to deal with a complex world. For students, we begin with building positive relationships. This means strategically and intentionally creating positive relationships with ALL students. Some of the basics of building a relationship include understanding the universal things that all people need in relationships like trust, validation, safety, and acceptance.

2. Where do we use universal SEL?

   Answer: Everywhere.

Consider implementing additional efforts in classrooms, playgrounds, the school bus, the lunchroom, and before and after school time. We should see universal SEL reflected in the way we organize and manage our classroom, how we speak to each other, and how we resolve disagreements.

3. When do we use universal SEL?

Answer: There are five different ways to integrate SEL. They are academic inclusion, everyday teaching practices, curriculum options, active skill building, and practices for adults. There are different times and places where each of these interventions is most appropriate. But they can and should be used throughout the day. Identify practices and make them sustainable. Set your implementation up for success, by planning for sustainable SEL practices. Academic inclusion is intentionally integrating these practices into your academic subject. Everyday teaching practices include daily practices and collected data on your practice. Curriculum or active skill building includes lessons conducted in a thoughtful and intentional way. Systemic integration includes time, training, discussion, practice, and modeling.

4. What universal SEL practices should I use?

Answer: Use universal practices that are *sequential, active, focused*, and *explicit* (SAFE). You will need as a team to identify practices and make them sustainable. A meta-analysis of 213 school-based universal SEL programs examined the practice of SAFE SEL interventions (Durlak et al., 2011). The researchers found that programs following all four recommended SAFE training procedures produced significant effects for all six outcomes: (1) social and emotional skills, (2) attitudes toward self and others, (3) positive social behaviors, (4) conduct problems, (5) emotional distress, and (6) academic performance, whereas programs not following SAFE achieved significant effects in only three areas— attitudes, conduct problems, and academic performance (Durlak et al., 2011).

- Sequential (use a connected set of activities to achieve skill development): first understand your own emotions, understand others' emotions may differ from yours, learn to actively listen, learn perspective taking, etc. to build the skills of empathy

- Active (use active forms of learning): conversation, modeling, role play, discussion

- Focused (develop personal or social skills): at a specific time to learn, practice, and model

- Explicit (have explicit personal or social goals): discuss here what we are learning and why

How to Build Educator Capacity

Understanding how to build educator capacity is important when working toward successful interventions and changes. For educators to be successful, they need time to learn specific practices. Your role should allow you to provide direct instruction in SEL practices that they can use in their classroom and throughout the school.

The process of cultivating social and emotional competencies has five components: learn, teach, model, practice, and support. Demonstrating to teachers that you have a clear plan on how you will frame your work will not only allow you to clarify your role to others but also provide you with the opportunity to gather support for your initiatives. Teachers need time, ownership, a growth mindset, support and scaffolding, and autonomy. Is this a norm in your building? If not, is this something that a coach can help to identify and mediate? Change is a process for the adults just as much for the students, especially if these changes are to really take effect and produce the outcomes of a positive school climate where students learn the skills to be productive and healthy citizens.

TASK: Ask your stakeholders what they want to learn

Give educational stakeholders a survey where they can guide the direction of the work. Below is an example of the results of a survey.

SELECTED STRATEGIES FOR CONTINUED PROFESSIONAL DEVELOPMENT

What strategies would you like to learn more about to continue your work?
25 responses

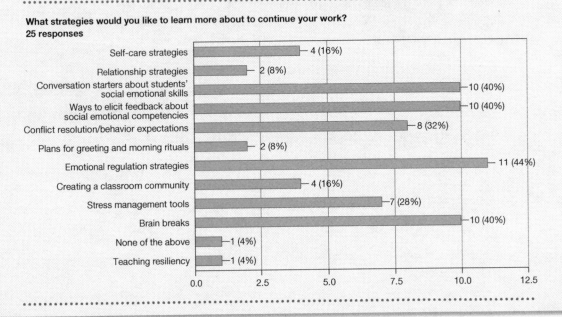

Preparing for Professional Development

As you consider all the information that will be helpful, you will want to build things that educators can easily understand, use, and adapt. Remember that they have a lot on their plate already. They should come away with information that is meaningful and can be used to enhance their practices. To educate educational stakeholders, include information about innovative procedures during implementation. Some examples could include teachable moments, application of skills in different areas of the school, problem-solving for specific groups, books used to discuss social and emotional skills, or videos created or used during implementation.

To enhance implementation and make it live in the school day to day, create action items for implementation with administration. This will include how to use materials for implementation, orientation plans, how to distribute curriculum materials, scheduled check-ins, and a support plan. The support plan may include follow-ups after the PD to help with specific challenges to implementation or the opportunity to give additional resources to the staff.

Professional development should be a flexible process. Feedback serves to inform the pacing of professional development. Are we going too fast? Does everyone feel supported in this work? It is up to schools to answer the questions: How would we collect? What is the flow of communication? What could it look like? What are the frequency and form? Communication of how you are structuring professional development lets stakeholders know that you hear them. If there is a problem of practice that seems to come up in the feedback, you collect and address it in the next professional development. Perhaps a flowchart will help ease communication. Building a flowchart can help illustrate these concepts or your path in a visual way for all schools to understand the process and learn the same intervention language.

We must do more to enhance professional development in and out of school settings. We have learned that the manuals are necessary but not sufficient. The train-the-trainer model does not provide enough support for individuals implementing this complex intervention. Workshops help to introduce concepts and increase knowledge but are not as helpful in continual implementation. Professional development should have a piece of consultation and coaching to connect the learning with practice. Allow teachers to talk to each other about their process and if possible, include a coach who can work side by side with the teachers or other professionals to strategize ways to implement SEL into the everyday life of their class.

- Needs assessment

- Clear targets or goals and teaching to those objectives

- Active learning strategies

- Visual techniques

- Monitoring and adjusting to the needs of the audience

- Feedback; practical applications

  - Training must include scenarios to walk through the process of intervention; it helps people to hear about real kids or cases and makes it more applicable for their own setting

Consider creating documents to support the things that they learned during their professional development—for example, a cheat sheet that has key concepts, especially when trying to integrate SEL into every day of your classroom. The cheat sheet may have prompts for what to look for and reminder sentences. It could contain brief strategies or your problem-solving processes. When learning any new skill, it is helpful to have reminders or cues to help educators. Some options include providing teachers with the ability to participate in PD: lead, co-teach, online, in person, in small groups, large groups, hands on, discussion, planning time. This would be a great way to include your SEL team members in professional development.

Intervention Practices as Described by Teachers

It is one thing for you or the administrators to know the purpose of the many interventions that schools use these days, but do teachers know? Can they define, connect it to practices, and summarize the rationale for using the practices? The stakeholders will have a better understanding of each intervention if they can label and define what each of them is meant to accomplish. This activity will help schools understand more about the specifics of each SEL-related current school-based intervention and include what practices are being used.

- Name of intervention/practice
- The official definition of intervention
- Practices: ways of being and doing including the relationship to Social Emotional Learning skills/competencies
- The rationale for using the intervention

INTERVENTION	DEFINITION	PRACTICES	RATIONALE OR "WHY"

Delivering Professional Development

Delivering professional development effectively is like any other skill; it takes practice to master. In my experience delivering professional development to teachers, afterschool personnel, counselors, bus drivers, administrators, families, and others, I have found three non-negotiables. Professional development needs to be meaningful, appropriate, and applicable. This is where knowing your audience is most helpful. Edit your professional development to the best and most succinct information so that the stakeholders can use that information. It must be meaningful to that specific group. Consider them asking: What's in it for me? Why do I need to give you my attention and active participation? Is it appropriate? I have been guilty of both giving too much information at one time and talking in acronyms. I learned that I need to understand what the audience already knows and scaffold that learning to educate them about the theory, principles, and details of the intervention. Discover what they need to know to practice the social emotional learning strategies in the classroom. Tailor the professional development to meet the specific needs of your audience. And finally, what is applicable? Am I giving the audience strategies and skills that they can use right away? Professional development is not meant to be a semester course like you would take in college. It is meant to disseminate key pieces of information and offer opportunities to continue to learn and grow through exercises and reflection.

Once the intervention is in full swing, professional development may change to reflect less education (sit and get) and more active participation. One strategy for brief professional development sessions is the following format: Accomplishments, Practice scenario, Brainstorm, Strategy, Feedback. This allows the stakeholders to take a more active role in discussing the intervention and using the skills for their specific class. It is not just the implementation of direct teaching of social and emotional skills to students. Professional development includes implicitly giving strategies for how the language of the intervention can be included in both daily routines and academic subjects.

TASK: Consider presentation of do's and don'ts

DO'S	DON'TS
• Demonstrate enthusiasm for the team	• Consider self-directed mixed grade-level teams (pros/cons)
• Plan for upcoming PD settings: questions and feedback	• Forget to honor the hard work and background that previous staff worked on
• Give samples	
• Recognize suggestions	• Talk about "kids these days"
• Offer to do more research if needed	• Call kids "low flyers, Tier 2 kids, that kid"
• Laugh/collegiality-proven membership in the group	• Excuse or omit data that is not favorable rather than owning it
• Provide meaningful handouts	
• Talk about personal history and background with new audiences	• Focus on one student or situation that others will not relate to
• Share relatable examples	• Forget to have a note taker
• Let them know it is okay to go slow	• Give articles to read during presentation time
• Be positive about teachers and principal	• Show too many videos

DO'S	DON'TS
• Be aware of the time	• Assume that there is a common definition for some terms. Some terms can mean different things to different people (e.g., respect)
• Frame presentation by starting with goals	
• Start with celebrations	• Use too many acronyms or omit definitions of the acronyms
• Share opportunities	
• Create a planning document, especially if more than one person presenting	
• Use movement to your advantage in exercises like gallery walk or switching groups	
• Plug other ways to be involved in the work	
• Discuss personal connection to the work as a coach	
• Walk around and make face-to-face connections	
• Make a Plan B for tech that doesn't work	
• Recognize if staff disconnected (e.g., grading papers, emailing, texting, talking)	
• Allow time for processing and interaction	

PHASE 2: PROFESSIONAL DEVELOPMENT ROLE TASKS

Choosing Interventions

Ideally, the interventions that you choose will be evidence-based. However, the process of determining how to implement is context dependent. For example, school 1 and school 2 decided to work on enhancing students' emotional regulation skills. School 1 gathered ideas from the students about what their stressors are, how they manage their stressors currently, and what suggestions they may have that could work. School 2 gathered input from the SEL team and then posted their ideas in the staffroom for staff members to comment on and add to. Both schools received input when designing the intervention, but *how* they did it was based on what they knew about their people.

When planning effective implementation strategies, keep the larger goal in mind of helping students and adults build capacity for social and emotional competencies. This will involve knowing your people, understanding their needs and challenges, choosing interventions that are meaningful, and problem-solving along the way. Embrace the challenges that you may experience and see them as opportunities to help promote positive change. Always remember that SEL can create long-term change for not just the school but also for students and their personal development and goals.

TASK: Understand and make clear to others why specific interventions were chosen and how they can engage in the process

Discuss with educational stakeholders:

- What is the intervention that was chosen?

- What is it meant to do?

- What does the research say?

- What outcomes should we expect?

- How will the educators give feedback about the intervention?

- How will students give feedback about the intervention?

Scaffold Trainings for Interventions Based on Their Role

The SEL coach's role is to help all educational stakeholders understand what social and emotional competencies are and why they are important in the school setting. This is also a time to provide clarity around what SEL is and is not and the reasons the school, classroom, or district is using resources for this effort.

TASK: Invest in different ways to help different stakeholders learn more about SEL

- Ask stakeholders to define SEL and determine if they need more direct instruction to narrow down the definitions.

- Teach educational stakeholders using different modalities: direct instruction, articles, newsletters, videos, group work, PLCs, observations, etc.

- Create materials for ease of use in defining and explaining SEL for each group of educational stakeholders. For example, the information you give to teachers will be much more complex and specific than with such groups as school secretaries or student resource officers.

Enhancing Classroom Procedures
After Professional Development

Partnering with teachers in the SEL coach role is one of the most effective ways to create sustainable change. You may want to focus on options and opportunities and those are often in the form of interventions. There are three different ways discussed here that you can provide coaching for teachers with SEL. They are brainstorming, data collection or observations, and modeling/demonstrating SEL practices.

Durlak and DuPre (2008) found that one of the most important characteristics of the implementation is compatibility or fit. The intervention needs to fit with the school or district's mission, priorities, and values. The SEL coach will work with stakeholders to determine fit of specific classroom procedures. A program may need to be modified to meet the unique needs of your school. (Durlak & DuPre, 2008).

TASK: Determine which process would work best to support your staff

Brainstorm with an individual teacher

1. Teacher requests help to determine the best ways to teach/model SEL practices in the classroom environment.

2. SEL implementer does two to three observations at different times to collect baseline data (use observation form).

3. Meet with the teacher to discuss the teacher's primary concern in delivering SEL to students.

4. Develop a plan that focuses on a social emotional competency in collaboration with the teacher.

5. Teach intervention to the teacher.

6. Teacher implements (alone or in collaboration with).

7. Select timeline for implementation and review.

8. The teacher collects data for progress monitoring.

9. Meet with the teacher to decide: What are the outcomes of the intervention? Is it meeting the teachers' immediate needs? If not, what needs to be changed? If so, what is the next need?

10. Create a plan with the teacher to educate other teachers about your process. PD, write-up steps, invite teachers into the classroom, etc.

(Continued)

(Continued)

Small group trial

1. A small group of teachers decides to try an intervention that focuses on enhancing student social and emotional competencies.

2. Staggered implementation (option): Training/Coaching starts with only one grade level, one class, one group of volunteer teachers with the expectation that more will be included in the next year or cycle.

3. Collect baseline data. If possible, the SEL implementer should do separate observations for each teacher in the group.

4. Determine objectives with a date for the date to review.

5. Discuss procedure: Make sure all teachers understand the importance of fidelity.

6. Implement intervention.

7. Each teacher collects progress-monitoring data. SEL implementer can also offer observations.

8. Review data from all teachers after implementation.

9. Decide next steps: If effective, will the teachers teach the larger group the intervention? If not effective, will they try another method?

Invite a teacher to model/demonstrate SEL practices

1. A teacher with excellent SEL practices is identified and asked if they are interested in providing PD to other teachers.

2. The SEL implementer does several observations to determine the most effective and teachable lessons or activities.

3. Collaborate with the teacher to understand their process.

4. Ask the teacher to talk about the procedure (PD/after school) and invite other teachers to watch their process.

PHASE 3: PROFESSIONAL DEVELOPMENT ROLE TASKS

Self-Reflection on Professional Development

Reflection has many facets; for example, reflecting on work enhances its meaning. Reflecting on experiences encourages insight and complex learning. This includes learning more about your ability to reflect on your professional development skills. It is important for adults to practice reflection and model it for the students. "Self-reflection and self-assessment are instructional tasks whereby teachers ask students to actively think about their own work. For students to self-reflect on their work, teachers should ask them to assess their own work. The process should not stop there, however; students also need to think about how to improve their work on the basis of their self-assessment. In order to assist students with this process, teachers need to develop goals and priorities with students" (Yoder, 2014a, p. 20). Reflection involves linking a current experience to previous learning. Educators can foster their growth when practicing reflection.

TASK: SEL coach to engage in a self-reflection process

- What was the most effective part of the PD?

- What was the least effective part of the PD?

- What was the staff reaction to the material?

- How will you plan to revisit these topics later?

- What was the most useful addition to the presentation? Posters, handouts, videos, shared materials, articles? Why did you feel it was useful?

Consider the things that did not go well, but don't beat yourself up about it. Every person who teaches adults will have at least one "bad" PD.

Learn From Others' Experiences Through an Exit Ticket

Exit tickets can help you learn more about the quality of your professional development. Learning what your audience is learning is vital to assessing the coach's efficacy of the coach expectation of providing professional development. It is important to have that information for you to follow up after presentations to have an action plan to help the attendees successfully use the new skills or ideas that were conveyed in the presentation. You can create action plans based on the information gathered from the exit ticket.

TASK: Design an exit ticket to understand more about what others learned

The questions to consider:

- What are your current experience and use of Social Emotional Learning?

- What did you find helpful about this training?

(Continued)

- Would you like more information or additional trainings? If so, in what areas?
- What resources do you need to help you continue with the work of SEL implementation?
- What are your next steps for continuing this work?
- Is there anything else that you would like to share?

Efficacy and Fidelity of Coaching Role

The SEL coach will want to measure whether the things they are teaching in professional development are having a real impact on the use of the selected competencies. It is particularly meaningful to understand the stages of skill development and determine how professional development has impacted attendees. Consider measuring and collecting data on skills in the following ways: skill awareness where the participant is knowledgeable about the skill necessary and how to use it; skill ability and confidence that are demonstrated by participants who can practice a specific skill in a practice setting; skill utilization, which is when the participant can use the skill in the intended setting; and finally, skill proficiency, which is the participants' use of the skill and ability to adapt it to different situations (Centers for Disease Control and Prevention, 2019). However you choose to measure the effectiveness of your professional development, make sure it is a regular part of your practice.

TASK: Determine the efficacy of professional development through skill ability, utilization, and proficiency

Conduct a pre-/post-assessment: before and after the professional development session

Pre-/Post-Assessment:

1. I do/do not (circle) feel able to teach _____ competency.

2. I can use/don't see how I can use (circle) _____
   competency during _____.

3. I feel competent (rate 1 = not at all to 5 = very ready) _____ about teaching
   _____ competency. And I do so in the following ways:

   _____

   _____

   _____.

PHASE 4: PROFESSIONAL DEVELOPMENT ROLE TASKS

Training Others

Unfortunately, there will be times when only a few people can attend an outside workshop or training. The SEL coach can magnify this training by asking those who attended the training to share with others one thing they learned. An example of training can include things like the creation of an intervention template review and SEL lesson reflection form, designing training for staff and parents, coding, and teaching the coaches their specific expertise and interventions.

TASK: Maximize outside trainings by training others

Each group will do the following for their section (20 minutes):

1. Describe it (can use PowerPoints or notes).

2. How does this inform your current work?

3. How can you use it in the future?

TOPIC	ITEMS TO POTENTIALLY COVER	SIGN UP

A Scope and Sequence Document

Your SEL team or district leadership may want to develop a scope and sequence document that can help educators teach the concepts on a predictable schedule. It can help with fidelity and sustainability in your system. The scope and sequence describe the ideas and concepts that will be covered in your SEL implementation. This can include a preselected curriculum or not. It describes the things that the students will be exposed to and learn during implementation. The scope and sequence need to be developmentally appropriate and sequential. This usually comes in a list format, with all topics listed in the order that they appear in the book or course. Scope describes the areas of development addressed in the implementation, while sequence refers to plans and content to support students' learning.

TASK: Create a scope and sequence document

Below is a question to help frame your discussions about what would be on your scope and sequence:

- What are the skills or competencies of focus?

- Write your scope and sequence statement. What are the results you would like to see?

- What strategies would you use to teach, model, and practice these skills?

- How will you arrange the content to meet your need of focus? Monthly or quarterly?

Determine Who Will Do What in Universal Implementation

When your school system has decided on practices, interventions, or a curriculum, it will be important to set training expectations in an action plan. It may be helpful to break these expectations down by role. This will also prepare the system for upcoming professional development needs.

TIMELINE	PRINCIPAL	SEL COACH	SEL TEAM	TEACHERS
May–June	• Principals who are currently implementing SEL meet to debrief on end of year • Participate in initial training at end of year • Consider SEL training at beginning of school year • Decisions for implementation: orientation and PD plan	• Meet to debrief in May • Work with administration to determine a plan for training in fall • Participate in initial training in spring • Distribute materials	• Review data to determine if additional buy-in for SEL is necessary • Assist in implementation as needed	• Participate in any training in spring • Review materials if received • Review scope and sequence
August	• Integrate PD into schedule • Review materials for principals • Order additional materials if needed	• Conduct whole school training (90 min: grade-level teamwork, intro to SEL, Scope and Sequence and Core program elements, resources) • Plan additional trainings for specialists	• Collect questions from grade-level teams about implementation • Assist with training (as needed)	• Attend training • Integrate scope and sequence into lesson plans • Schedule demo lessons from the SEL coach if needed
First month	• Plan for check-in after the fourth week • Include slide for curriculum night • Schedule training for EAs and other support staff	• Formally or informally check in on teachers to assess needs • Provide differentiated support based on student needs	• Continue to gather feedback from staff about implementation	• Begin lessons • Reach out if there are questions • Send blurbs about SEL in newsletters • Include parent resources
Mid-year	• Consider PTSA or parent groups in education of SEL	• Formally or informally check in on teachers to assess needs	• Determine if supplemental social emotional learning lessons are needed to support current implementation	• Newsletter blurbs can contain problem-solving steps, calm-down strategies, and emotion management skills

(Continued)

(Continued)

TIMELINE	PRINCIPAL	SEL COACH	SEL TEAM	TEACHERS
End of year	• Evaluate process and tweak if necessary • Plan for trainings of new staff for next year	• Formally survey the teachers to assess implementation	• Evaluate learning and needs for next year's implementation	• Evaluate lessons and collaborate in problem-solving to make implementation better
Ongoing throughout year	• Continued focus and time for teachers to work on Social Emotional Learning • Braid together SEL with other initiatives	• Individual support for supplemental materials, pacing, planning, etc. • Provide supplemental materials (books, etc.) • Training for teachers, EA, specialists, parents • Use the problem-solving process to determine needs for building • Assist teachers in creating templates for newsletters	• Use the problem-solving process to determine needs for building	• Complete 15 lessons by the end of the year • Reinforce lessons in other subjects • Participate in data gathering and evaluation of lessons and resources

JEFF BECKER

....

SEL coach/Speaker/Curriculum Developer

Florida

Interview:

1. *What was most effective about your practice there? What do you feel got you the most bang for your buck?*

   The most bang for my buck, as far as practical things that we did as a team? The foundational knowledge was huge—the frequency in providing clarity for what social emotional learning is to adults. This meant educating them through professional development, one on one in the coach role, or helping to build capacity in the team to train others. Strengthening the inner circle's understanding of SEL and having that trickle down to the staff.

2. What didn't work?

The biggest waste of time during that program implementation was I should've spent more time with transparency of our processes and procedures that we were using for an SEL approach to discipline. Yes, this kid will receive discipline according to our code of conduct, but we are also going to love this kid and it will take a ton of time. To be friends with the kid, to learn more about their life, to build a relationship with the kid so that we can actually give them the SEL tools. What was happening, what people saw was that these bad kids are getting away with everything. That took our program a few steps back. When they saw us pulling the kid to talk or I would be having a game of catch with one of the boys in the schoolyard while I was talking to them, some teachers would think, "The bad kids get special treatment." And I remember saying to a teacher, "They do! You have no idea what this student has been through; he just needs more than some of the other kids." The object is the restoration of the relationship.

3. What did the role of principal mean for you to be able to get things done with SEL?

I have been in polar opposite situations. It depends on the administrator. For some it just wasn't in the principal's core. They thought I am going to hammer these kids with reading for them to be successful in school. I am going to put a laminated paper on the in-school suspension that says restorative justice center and kids are going to sleep in there. So, it doesn't matter how many laminated pieces of paper are in the school. I have also had principals who talk the talk but don't walk the walk. The principal understanding is huge. The principal needs to actually be bought in—that is one of the biggest factors.

4. What happens if you don't have teacher buy-in?

Teacher apprehension is caused when people don't feel prepared for something; they view it as a threat. If you don't prepare teachers and make them feel comfortable with something, and make sure they know what things are and are not, then they will view it as a threat and they will reject it. Almost the easiest part is when you have the one outlier who is raising their hand every seven minutes; she is not the threat. It is just overall staff apprehension. How do you lower that apprehension? And the inner circle—half of my SEL team—couldn't give you a clear definition of what the philosophy of SEL was. They *knew it was good, they knew they were in for it, and they were committed to it because it was happy and right. But as far as the understanding, we needed to go a lot deeper with it.*

5. *When half of your key leaders did not have the understanding of SEL, what did that mean?*

   You need to defend your initiative at some level. The people who are there at a superficial level will not be true champions of the program. They are not going to be able to look at those people who are misunderstanding your program and actually knowledgeably defend, explain, and teach why this way is a better way. You are going to need it to build capacity in the early days when it just looks like fluff. When a team doesn't understand SEL, the staff can see when members of the inner circle don't really know. The more people understand it, the more they can move the culture down the field.

6. *If you were to do the implementation over again, would you do anything differently?*

   The tension is always market share. What happens when things go sideways is people get scared and revert to your automatic responses. What happens in schools when test scores come in and the principal is not thrilled with them? The first thing that gets canceled is the SEL professional development that I have scheduled to do. I probably got wiped off the training board five or six times over the course of a year. When things go sideways, the SEL meeting that the administrator is supposed to be at is the first thing that gets cut. When leaders become fearful, what I have observed is that we cut the fluff and they just want to bang down on the academics. If I could do it over again, maybe I would have that conversation and say, "Hey, this year this is probably going to happen in the first quarter of the year you're going to get back standardized test results, and you're going to go, oh crap, or the first round of formative assessments are going to come back and you're going to go, Oh my gosh." Whatever it is, it's just going to happen and the first thing that you're going to want to do is cut into this social emotional learning time. You're going to want to take over a staff meeting because you're going to "need to address something with the staff." My advice is to catch leaders early on before these things happened, proactive, and say, Hey this year is going to be rocky with us here with your brand new reading program and things are going to come up. Maybe, to get a commitment, do I have your word that SEL is not going to be the thing that suffers for it? If you catch them before those things happen in a sober moment, they're going to do what is right. They might think twice before wiping you off the professional development board.

7. *What do you view as successful contributions that you made to the system?*

Leading meaningful meetings and building capacity with that inner circle. This is what I would tell somebody if I knew they were going to go into it. Don't be afraid to teach your team because when I did, they thanked me, which was great. I did a little 5- or 10-minute training on what happens in the fear center of the brain. They felt that to be a really great conversation. But sometimes I felt apprehensive that these meetings are not for me teaching. If you create things that are easy for the teachers to use, it is the spoonful of sugar. It's creating something easy and so whether it's curriculum or whether you're it yourself, I would say honor your teachers by setting them up for success. There's nothing worse for a teacher that would be set up to fail. Make it easy for the teachers, a slam dunk. And celebrate them when they hit it out of the park. Easy win.

8. *When you think of the future of Social Emotional Learning in your system or your work, what gives you a sense of hope? What makes you concerned or worried?*

I'm hopeful because I'm really encouraged by the amount of people that are excited about it and states are starting to mandate SEL. I see tons of principals around the country who are jazzed up about it. They're genuinely excited when I'm doing these professional developments. I think I did about nine last month and teachers are so on board and they're so thankful. I think about other things I've done professional development on, and I could just feel the negative energy. But not with this. They get it, and they understand it they're genuinely in for it. The thing that makes me afraid is that it is the Wild West and there's no regulation for every misguided program and platform and person and they're just getting it wrong. It's just blatantly wrong and it's giving an SEL a bad name.

CHAPTER 8

....

ADVANCE YOUR PRACTICE

Coaching

Coaching is central to the name SEL coach. But it is often the responsibility that takes the most time to master. In fact, it may take a year or two for the SEL coach to do some of the things that are required because coaching requires a tremendous amount of trust. This is especially a challenge for those who are new to the building and require some time to build relationships before teachers feel comfortable having them observe and give feedback on their teaching and modeling of social and emotional competency.

Coaches are key to producing positive outcomes. The seminal 2002 study by Joyce and Showers found that the combination of training, presentation/lecture, demonstration plus practice, coaching administrative support, and data feedback produces an effectiveness rate of 95% in the knowledge of content, skill implementation, and classroom implementation. What researchers found was that training via presentation or demonstration is not enough. There is insufficient post-training consultation. We just train and hope it will happen. It was found that traditional, short-term, didactic, isolated events only provide 14% evidence of effectiveness (Joyce & Showers, 2002).

PHASE 1: SEL COACH ROLE TASKS

Clarity for the Coaching Role

One of the primary questions you may have to answer for your educational stakeholders is "Why"? Why SEL in general and, more specifically, why an SEL coach? Explaining to the educational stakeholders why SEL and system changes are important will invest others in positive changes. To encourage investment, frame your proposals using 5Ws and one H. In Phase 1 you will help the educational stakeholders with the why and who. The "why" was elaborated in Phase 1 of the leadership role and the first three chapters of this book. In Phase 1 of the SEL coach role, you will be tasked to introduce yourself and the expectations of the role by staff.

- Why SEL and an SEL coach?
- Who you are?
- What do you do?
- Where do you do it?
- When do you do it?
- How do you do it?

Each of these areas provides important context about your role and about SEL in general as your colleagues and leadership begin to build trust in you and your work. Having a clear plan on how you will frame your work will not only allow you to clarify your role to others but also provide you with the opportunity to gather support for your initiatives. As an SEL coach, you'll need to be able to successfully invest others in the idea that SEL and SEL coaching are both necessary and effective.

TASK: Create a brief document that explains these things to get clarity for everyone

How would you answer these questions?

Why SEL and an SEL coach?

_____

_____

_____

Who are you?

_____

_____

_____

What do you do?

_____

_____

_____

Where do you do it?

_____

_____

_____

When do you do it?

_____

_____

_____

How do you do it?

_____

_____

_____

Getting Administration Feedback on Coaching

It is important to understand administrators' perspectives on the coaching part of your role. Work with administrators to determine what parts of coaching the staff are mandatory vs. voluntary. Leadership can demonstrate their support by letting teachers choose how they interact with the SEL coach. For example, coaching, observations, data collection in the classroom, and being part of the team should be considered voluntary. While receiving trainings and communication is part of the whole school structure, the hope is that coaches can demonstrate their worth and needs as they build relationships and demonstrate how their learning can affect the educational stakeholders' processes. "Learning is about stepping out of the known and into the unknown, and coaches depend on the principal to put pressure on teachers through a clearly articulated vision" (Sweeney, 2011, p. 158).

After surveying administrators, there are qualities that they appreciate in the coaching role. Administrators appreciate a coach with the skill to follow through and support staff. This role was helpful to provide structured opportunities for staff to engage in positive relationships and brought SEL into staff conversations. They wanted SEL coaches who supported individual teachers with observations and feedback, modeled positive relationship building, and sought opportunities to engage with students and staff. SEL coaches who care and really want to help with solutions promote a positive culture by thinking we are all in this together. Other attributes include being super accessible and approachable, making it seem doable. The responsibility of an SEL coach is to be organized, a good listener, someone who tries hard, reflective, and efficient. Another strategy that administrators appreciate is to provide blurbs for educational stakeholders on a regular basis with tips to follow up.

TASK: Interview administration about where they see the role of the coach

What are your priorities as part of the coach role?

_____

_____

_____

What coaching models have you seen as being successful with your staff?

_____

_____

_____

What are some efficient ways to build trusting relationships with the staff?

_____

_____

_____

A Letter to Introduce the Coach Role With Teachers

You may want to consider writing a letter of introduction of yourself and your role if you are new to the school. While it may seem formal, it can go a long way in answering some questions that teachers have right off the bat.

Dear Colleagues,

I am so thrilled to have been selected as the SEL Coach at Example School. I'm eager to join your team and partner with you all in our quest for the success of each student. My primary role is to help you with the strategies to enhance student social and emotional competencies. This will be done through training, coaching, and problem-solving collaboratively with teachers, parents, and staff. I will recommend the use of evidence-based strategies, collaborate with you, and problem-solve around tools to support social emotional skill development. My role is a full-time position. I will keep my weekly schedule posted on my office door in the main office. A little bit about my background. . . .

I sincerely hope that our time together will be filled with lots of joy mixed in with the hard work we do each day for kids. During the first weeks of school, I would like to invite you to schedule an informal meeting with me either individually or as a grade-level team. The format and who is included are up to you. It is important to me that I learn from all of you about how I can best support you and your students. Further, I am eager to learn all about you, both professionally and personally, as building relationships is a core value for me as a coach. I have an open-door policy and want you to feel welcome to come and talk with me for any reason. I'm looking forward to working in collaboration with all of you to continue to build a community that will achieve great things for each student.

Please feel free to reach out anytime via email or call.

Best regards,

Your Name

SEL Coach

Example School

What areas do you need to address in this letter?

- What is your personal why for SEL? How does it mesh with the district or school and why?

- Who are you? How do you establish your expertise? What previous experiences have you had that led you to this role?

- What are some of the things that you could briefly explain about your role?

- Where and how can you be reached?

- What are some hopes for working with staff and students?

Introductions Matter: Working With Stakeholders

Since much of your time will likely be working with teachers, it will be important to answer their questions and be as transparent about what you can and cannot do to help them with SEL implementation. This is particularly true with the coaching part of your role.

For an SEL coach to be effective, we must be able to answer most of these questions. With anything new to your system, there is a level of skepticism. If it is not done thoughtfully, teachers can feel that they are on their own in figuring out how to do this. And this can cause stress and even burnout. They need to understand their responsibility and the things that they can lean on the SEL coach for. In what ways can teachers partner with their SEL coach to help them during implementation? Teachers will feel better about engaging in new practices if they feel supported. And that includes providing the space to be autonomous. Allowing a range of practices that will meet these needs can help to accomplish this. Then teachers are doing what they feel comfortable with while remaining accountable for teaching SEL.

Over the years of doing this work, there are a few types of questions that are often asked:

- About the SEL coach role: What will this look like? Will the coach work with individual students? If so, how will the students be selected? How much time will the coach be in classrooms? Does the coach have classroom experience as a teacher? How often will the coach be in our building?

- About time: Do we start in the fall? How can we figure all of this out before the school year begins? When will we have time for training? When will this happen? How do we make time to fit everything into our busy schedules? Will we have enough time to teach this explicitly?

- About an SEL curriculum: Will there be an SEL curriculum? If there is a curriculum, will we be trained? Who will train us? What if we are using something that already works? Will I have to change what I am currently doing? Will this consist of isolated lessons? Do I have to do them all? What will this look like? What does the model look like?

- About parent/families: What do the parents/families know about SEL and our implementation? What happens if we don't get parental support for this? How do we know what parents need support with?

Observations: What Is the Precedence?

A classroom observation might be a little different than some of the student-focused observations that most educators are used to. Observations include sitting in the room with the class going on as usual. The observer records the date, time, class/teacher, total students in class, total adults, ratios, how the students are seated, what type of lesson, type of teaching style (transition, large group lecture, small group, independent work, read aloud, read silently, instructional game, media, whole class carpet time), observed behavior tally (off task, out of seat, talk out, noncompliant, other). They record each event and behavior of the whole class as it occurs to get a sense of the class dynamic not just the identified child. They also review notes and develop themes and patterns to explore with the teacher.

Before you conduct classroom observations, make sure it is expected and wanted. Many teachers will not want someone they hardly know observing the classroom even if you are not evaluating them. Some believe that having someone walk in at a random time to observe pulls them away from focusing on the kids. Take the time to understand the teachers' feelings before entering the classroom for observation.

The goal is to meet teachers where they are. Different teachers will have different needs before, during, and after the observation. Some teachers request feedback and a copy of observation notes. Some feedback sessions have been both coaching and teaching. You might bring in additional tools (e.g., a story for class, a lesson for addressing behavior, etc.) and/or something for the teacher to do differently with the classroom. Some are looking for help/ideas on working with students. Others would like to go over the data the coach collected and then brainstormed ideas for working with the student. Teachers may need positive, quick problem-solving for student interventions. Some prefer getting some recommendations after hearing what kind of support they wanted. Sometimes the coach may email based on the need and the teacher's preference. For some SEL coaches, it works to leave a note pointing out positive things that they observed. Teachers may choose to meet one on one in your office or in the classroom after school or during teacher prep time. It will be the SEL coaches' goal to learn more about the precedence and preference for observations and drop-ins.

TASK:Determine the precedence set for the SEL coach to go into classrooms

- Are you only allowed to go into classrooms when invited?

- Is a drop-in culture already established?

- Would a Google sign-in sheet to request a visit work for your staff?

- What do teachers need to know about the observation process to make it more accessible for them? One example is a template that describes what ways you are supporting others to give teachers an idea of how you can help them.

Assess Your Adult SEL

One of the most crucial parts of the SEL implementation process is to build adult capacity to teach, model, and support social and emotional competencies. It is the SEL coaches' responsibility to work with staff to promote teaching practices that encourage social and emotional competencies.

In your coaching work, it might be helpful to focus on the teaching practices that support SEL. These practices can often be observed in the classroom setting. The Center on Great Teachers and Leaders identified 10 teaching practices that promote social, emotional, and academic skills (Yoder, 2014a). These 10 practices can be used in classrooms to support positive learning environments, social emotional competencies, and academic learning (Yoder, 2014a). They comprise social teaching practices including student-centered discipline, teacher language, responsibility and choice, and warmth and support. Instructional teaching practices are cooperative learning, classroom discussions, self-assessment and self-reflection, balanced instruction, academic press and expectations, and competence building (Yoder, 2014a).

To implement these practices successfully, teachers must strengthen their own social and emotional skills. To model and encourage positive student interactions, teachers themselves need the social and emotional skills required to communicate effectively with students and to handle stressful situations that can occur in classrooms (Brackett et al., 2009). Teachers who are socially and emotionally competent develop supportive relationships with students, create activities that build on the strengths of students, and help students develop the basic social and emotional skills necessary to participate in classrooms (Jennings & Greenberg, 2009). In my work, I often use these teaching practices to illustrate how SEL is more than a curriculum taught on a schedule. These teaching practices support the practice and use of SEL.

TASK: Assess teaching practices that support SEL and staff SEL competencies

- Self-Assessing Social and Emotional Competencies
  - Use this link https://bit.ly/3G8Mxj5
  - Consider which practices are currently happening in your school. Are there any that you would like to focus on?

PHASE 2: SEL COACH ROLE TASKS

In Phase 2 of the SEL coach role, you will deepen your practice by adding some tools and reflections for what you do, where you do it, when you do it, and how you will do it.

What Can the SEL Coach Do to Support Staff Through Coaching?

Discover different types of coaching; these are points of contact. How will your teachers need you to partner with them? What has proven successful to provide their own expertise and skills in teaching SEL to other educators? Teachers can demonstrate their proficiency to other staff through multiple avenues such as professional development sessions that they design, a drop-in afterschool period, or during a team meeting. Another coaching model uses the role of a facilitator, where the teacher requests help and the coach builds capacity. SEL coaches can also be available to troubleshoot, working to support teachers in building whole class SEL lessons that are effective. The coach can help facilitate the adoption and use of a specific training curriculum.

For many coaches, determining how you will work with teachers in a coaching capacity is an evolving process. The roles will take shape over time. It will be important to provide check-ins to see if the coaching needs of staff change over time.

Here are some other collaboration points between the SEL coach and staff:

1. Brainstorming: Schedule a meeting with the coach to share student concerns and consider what supports and interventions might be appropriate. This may result in classroom observation and follow-up, a referral to the student evaluation team, and/or recommendations for universal interventions or to consult with other staff.

2. Classroom observation and debrief: The coach observes concerns within the setting (classroom, specials, lunch, recess) making notes of student behaviors and environmental factors. A debrief meeting is scheduled to talk about what was observed and brainstorm ideas for universal interventions.

3. Modeling universal intervention strategies: The coach provides evidence-based universal classroom strategies. The coach may model the use of these strategies in the classroom.

4. Problem-solving in relationship building: Work with the coach to problem-solve, maintain, and/or restore a positive relationship with a student or group of students.

5. Consult on the student evaluation team: Consult with the coach regarding a possible referral to the team. The coach may assist with data collection for the referral.

6. Data collection tools: The coach may provide initial data collection and progress monitoring tools and assist with the use of these tools in the classroom.

TASK: Create a form for coaching support

This form will need to be unique to your culture.

Name: _____

Dates/times available to meet:

_____

_____

What is the purpose?

_____

_____

What should the SEL coach prepare for our collaboration?

- ☐ Brainstorming
- ☐ Classroom observation and debrief
- ☐ Modeling universal intervention strategies
- ☐ Problem-solving in relationship building
- ☐ Consult on a student evaluation
- ☐ Data collection tools

Other information for the SEL coach:

_____

Where Should You Engage in the Work of SEL Coaching?

We use social and emotional competencies when engaging with our colleagues, students, and families. The where is everywhere. And to be able to do that, we must focus on the skill sets of the adults. This is where adult SEL plays a vital role.

Teachers are instrumental in the execution and impact of SEL (Elbertson et al., 2010). Important for effective SEL implementation are the attitudes and beliefs teachers have about SEL in general and their ability to implement the program and model the behavior it intends to change in children (Elbertson et al., 2010).

TASK: Connect the social and emotional competencies with individual skills

Identify social and emotional competencies that your teachers want to work on and check in during individual coaching sessions.

COMPETENCIES	
• Integrating personal and social identities	• Understanding the influence of organizations/systems on behavior
• Identifying one's emotions and triggers	• Developing positive relationships
	• Demonstrating cultural competency

(Continued)

COMPETENCIES	
• Identifying personal, cultural, and linguistic assets	• Practicing teamwork and collaborative problem-solving
• Demonstrating honesty and integrity	• Resolving conflicts constructively
• Experiencing self-efficacy (belief in the ability to accomplish goals)	• Communicating effectively
• Linking feelings, values, and thoughts	• Showing leadership in groups
• Examining prejudices and biases	• Seeking or offering support and help when needed
• Reflecting on one's role to promote personal, family, and community well-being	• Standing up for the rights of others
• Evaluating personal, interpersonal, community, and institutional impacts	• Demonstrating curiosity and open-mindedness
• Anticipating and evaluating the consequences of one's actions	• Identifying solutions for personal and social problems
• Recognizing how critical thinking skills are useful both inside and outside of school	• Learning to make a reasoned judgment after analyzing information, data, and facts

How Can the SEL Coach Work With Educational Stakeholders?

There is no more crucial relationship than the one between the coach and the teacher in the implementation work. If we can get one teacher to begin implementing social and emotional practices as part of their regular ways of being and teaching, we could potentially impact hundreds of students over the years. This relationship must be built on trust and understanding, knowing the teachers, and determining what their strengths and challenges are. This includes both qualities that affect the practices in the classroom (such as cooperative teaching)—practices that affect the way they team (including things like PLC)—and outside the classroom (the way they manage their stress). Another part of building trust is to meet teachers where they are. Some teachers will be happy to collaborate with you and feel good about looking at their practices and potentially trying to change them. Other teachers will be resistant and may even misunderstand your intentions to help them.

A coach may identify a need from the teachers and help develop solutions for all. They may make a video to illustrate the procedure, observe a classroom, work with the teacher's current technology to make use of interventions more seamless, create a flipchart, model a lesson, or do other activities.

Your coaching role is both collaborative and innovative. When you work in a role of a coach, you will work directly with staff within the school community to ensure that teachers and administrators have the support they need to implement successful interventions. Coaching is about direct communication methods that help us understand the strengths and needs of educators. It can also include asking them to try something different. The coaching piece of your role is often about understanding the ways of thinking of the person you are coaching and meeting them where they are. One communication skill that will help with your coaching is to keep the educator from getting defensive by understanding them. This includes staying focused on the non-verbals of what people are saying as well as asking questions that don't make people feel defensive. This includes monitoring your use of the word *why*. For example, asking a teacher, "Why did you use that strategy?" *Why* can sometimes be perceived as an accusation or questioning of one's character. Starting a question with *why* can be useful, but it can also be interpreted poorly, which will derail your true intentions of getting more information about how the situation can be mediated. If *why* is the only response that comes to you in the moment, take a beat. Pausing is your friend unless safety is a consideration. Take a moment to think about a different way to ask the question without the deadly *why*. Instead, try an open-ended question like, how might you? Reflecting on this lesson, what worked and what could you tweak? What are your ideas about . . . ?

Here is an example coaching interaction:

Example coaching interaction:

SEL COACH:	How are you doing with your class this year?
TEACHER:	Overloaded; it is not fair that all problem kids have been thrown in my class.
SEL COACH:	It sounds like you are feeling that there are kids in your class who are demonstrating difficult behaviors and skills deficits. As you reflect on the first two weeks, what specific behavior stood out to be problematic?
TEACHER:	The students don't listen, get out of their seats, and talk out of turn.
SEL COACH:	Your expectations are not being met by the students. Which expectation gives you the most concern? What might you start with?

(Continued)

(Continued)

TEACHER:	Getting out of seats because when they move around, they interrupt me and their classmates.
SEL COACH:	Ok, so the students leaving their seats without permission. What do you think the cause of that behavior is?
TEACHER:	I don't know; they are just fidgety and unable to pay attention. They get up to sharpen their pencil, talk with their classmates, and ask to go to the bathroom.
SEL COACH:	What might be some strategies you could try?
TEACHER:	I don't have any strategies.
SEL COACH:	Is there anything that has worked for you in the past to address this issue?
TEACHER:	I think I will write their names on the board and keep them in at recess.
SEL COACH:	Some teachers find that students are struggling with stamina at this time of the year. Which strategies might help with that?
TEACHER:	I think I can try the brain breaks that you suggested at our last meeting.
SEL COACH:	That sounds great. Would you like any help implementing the intervention?

While learning to communicate this way can be overwhelming at first, it is a place to begin. All experience begins with a lack of experience. Just as the system grows and develops, so can you.

TASK: Practice collaborative conversations (reflection)

Practice Scenarios: What would you say in these situations to provide assistance?

- An elementary teacher, Ms. Brown, has a problem managing five girls who have demonstrated a pattern of being "mean" to other girls in the class.

- Your principal wants to address the results of the universal at Example Middle School. She is specifically concerned that a high percentage of students reported, "I am nervous in new situations. I easily lose confidence."

- There is a reoccurring problem with several fourth-grade boys roughhousing during recess.

- Jason, a first-grade student, is struggling with keeping his hands to himself at carpet time in class.

- Mr. Garcia, a seventh-grade science teacher, says he has done all the classroom management techniques and claims that "these kids today just don't care about learning."

When Is Coaching Appropriate?

When preparing the system for new interventions, it is important to work closely with those in the administration to ensure that specific goals are being met. Making sure the system is ready means that everyone has a better chance of success. As an SEL coach, your goals should be centered around long-term change and effects. When thinking about your implementation, it is vital to consider who will be working for and with you. Working together to create a sustainable plan means having people who believe in change and are open to lasting changes for positive effects. The first step is to determine the coaching model that best fits your school or district. There will need to be a menu of options to train stakeholders including time during the school day in whole school meetings, meeting before or after school, teamwork, small groups, and individuals. The strategies are there to determine capacity, troubleshoot when there is an issue, receive data, and facilitate the adoption and use of specific strategies. Of course, both the SEL coach and the teacher will have to allow for flexibility in this process This is not a predetermined checklist or something that has a strict timeline. You will need to understand more about how to co-lead with a teacher to give both of you ownership of the process. The relationship must be highly collaborative to allow for the openness to take on new practices that they might have to learn. The great thing about this work is that you get to learn from other educators from different backgrounds. Everyone you will work with brings different levels of expertise.

Ideas for when to work with staff:

1. Drop-in observations: This is a practice that is effective but should be used with caution and teachers' permission and based on the norms of the school. It will be important to ascertain a few things before dropping in to do an observation. Does the school culture support this practice? Does the individual teacher support drop ins? And are they open to feedback? Then continue to follow up with these teachers on occasion and offer them your support where needed. If a teacher is on board, leave them with something that you learned during your time in the class. With that level of communication, teachers will reach out to try new strategies recommended.

2. Scheduled cycle of observations: Meet with the teacher to go over the data you collected and the ideas you brainstormed for working with the class. You may choose to go over the data and ideas but not give them the observation notes. Or you can do a full cycle with a preconference, observation, follow-up conference, and then come back in a week to follow up with another cycle. Set up a time to meet with the teacher after to discuss the observation. Ask them how they thought it went and then share some great things they saw and ideas they could try. Then ask them if they wanted to try the strategy and if they wanted you to model it for them. Check in regularly to see if they need more help.

3. Schedule time to co-teach specific techniques: During discussion, you can arrive at some things to try. You may want to bring in additional tools and/or something for the teacher to do differently with the classroom. Then, follow up. There are some who are working on tasks in the room, while you can more deeply work with other teachers. Then, set up a "conference" with the teacher who has been working independently for a couple of weeks to see how it is going.

4. Brief check-ins: Meet one on one in an office, in the classroom after school, during teacher prep time, or in writing by email. You can have a quick discussion with a teacher, observe, and then arrange a post-discussion, but depending on the need/situation, it is not always this clean. It is common to have ongoing post-discussions, but swing back by a few days later to see how things are going.

It will also be helpful to get additional information about that process after working with teachers. It is important to learn if your feedback was valued. And did you learn anything about yourself in this process? Getting feedback can include sharing resources and ideas, building on current systems in the classroom, and so forth.

TASK: Share the good stuff

It is important to reflect on the staff's use of practices. You may want to consider optimizing these opportunities to instruct others in the group. It will be valuable to keep a list of the "good stuff" that you see they can do to have them teach and help colleagues and use that information to give them a "shout out" or "share out" with the group.

To find the practices that work well, consider the following:

What are staff doing well?

_____

_____

How can you acknowledge it?

_____

_____

Would they be willing to share?

_____

_____

PHASE 3: SEL COACH ROLE TASKS

Building Collaborative Relationships Through Empowerment

The goal for SEL coaches is to empower the educational stakeholders they work with. The purpose of your time as a coach is not to deliver whole class lessons regularly but to help teachers develop the skills and comfort level to do so themselves. You will work with teachers to coach, give resources, promote skill development, and develop strategies to do the teaching. Coaches must also have capacity-building goals and plans to increase their learning year over year.

Some of the biggest challenges as the coach is to overcome the perceptions that may happen when there is a lack of clarity and understanding of the coaching role. Teachers may not choose to use coaches to their intended capacity due to fear of being judged or evaluated. Teachers can feel like they have a limited amount of time, and that time can be more effectively used elsewhere. There can be miscommunication between what a coach can do (focus on universal prevention/intervention) and what the teacher would like them to do in that moment (e.g. substituting, recess duty, coaching one child, etc.). Principals can play a major role in helping ease that communication about what a coach does and does not do. And teachers who have been coached by you can help to ease others' reluctance by telling their stories to others. SEL coaches should be empowered as professionals, but they are not evaluators. And that point should be clear and communicated often.

Brainstorm: What are some key phrases that can be used to coach rather than evaluate a teacher? What are some examples of words not to use in coaching situations?

_____

_____

_____

_____

Nonevaluative Feedback Through Observation

The SEL coach is tasked to apply a collaborative approach when working with the staff by developing relationships, observing teachers, and providing resources. They are not to be perceived as an evaluator in their role. They are there to model/teach behavioral and social emotional interventions, provide professional development, and collaborate with the teachers.

The SEL coach may consider using a form like the one below to illustrate their observations. They would record the times throughout the observation in 2–5-minute increments, any observations about the social and emotional competencies of the kids, and any reflections or questions they may have while observing. The SEL coach and teacher can go over the form, or the coach may choose one specific question or practice to focus on because of the observation.

OBSERVATION FORM

Teacher: _____ Date: _____

Observer: _____

Lesson/technique/activity observed: _____

_____

_____

_____

_____

_____

_____

_____

_____

TIME	OBSERVATIONS	REFLECTIONS/ QUESTIONS

Ownership of SEL Implementation

Engaging teachers is critically important in this work. There are many ways to engage them: starting with involvement with shared vision and goals; providing them with leadership opportunities that are meaningful; and determining how they can help design methods for helping the rest of the staff learn how to teach and model SEL. Of course, teachers are crucial in creating a positive, supportive school culture. What do they see as the priorities for that? They can also benefit from instructional leadership that provides feedback. The SEL coach and teacher can work together to innovate the best way to integrate SEL into their specific classroom within the larger context of the school.

TASK: Developing a sense of ownership in SEL implementation

- Do the teachers feel like they are active participants or passive recipients of coaching?
- Are coaches enhancing leadership of teachers by engaging them in leader roles?
- How can the SEL coach provide differentiation for teacher needs?

How to Build Teacher Capacity

One of the fundamentals of student-centered teaching is supporting social and emotional growth. It includes things such as educating the "whole child" and building strong relationships with students (Cervone & Cushman, 2012). Teachers have a general understanding of the importance of "whole child" interventions. And it will have to include intentional actions and specific interventions to make that happen. Intentional actions include building relationships, creating engaging environments, meeting the students where they are, working to provide them with advisement to meet their individual needs, and promoting student reflection and awareness of the educators' own behaviors. This is in tandem with specific interventions to teach, model, practice, and support social and emotional skills. It will be important to be reflective about each strategy that the teacher uses.

TASK: Use a written format to have teachers think through the use of specific strategies. Ask the questions

- Briefly describe the strategy.
- How does the strategy work?
- How could you use the strategy in your classroom?
- Describe to a partner how you can use this strategy in the following week.

PHASE 4: SEL COACH ROLE TASKS

Maintaining Confidentiality in Coaching Conversations

It is best to be transparent when we are working with teachers. However, there may be situations where the teacher does not want the administrator to know that they are working with the SEL coach. That would be an area you would want to explore. Is there a break in communication or trust between the teacher and principal? Principals may want to be hands-on with the coaches to get a better feel for what they are doing day to day. Have the confidentiality discussion with principals. The hope is that they will understand why a teacher may request anonymity. For an SEL coach, this can be a tough road to walk. The rule of thumb is to rely on your ethical standards to guide you.

TASK: Reflection about expectations in your SEL coach role

Reflect on how to maintain confidentiality in coaching conversations:

How do we maintain confidentiality?

_____

_____

Will you share with the administration your coaching topic and practice with specific teachers?

_____

_____

What is your plan for sharing with administrators without breaking teacher confidentiality?

_____

_____

Working Through Resistance

We must focus on building teacher capacity to implement SEL in their classrooms and everyday interactions. This will require us to focus on how we can support teachers in feeling good about looking at their practices and taking a risk. Learned helplessness can emerge when an individual or group of individuals feel powerless to make any real change, which can lead to passivity, decreased interest, and burnout (Greer & Wethered, 1984). Learned helplessness can occur when teachers express low expectation of success in efforts, allowing roadblocks to stop progress toward stated goals, and ascribing success to factors beyond their control.

Because SEL coaches do not have authority over teachers and do not act as an evaluator, their ability to build trusting relationships is fundamental to teachers' investment in the SEL implementation and selected interventions. Engage principals and educational leaders to support your role and the interventions by ensuring that staff receive sufficient training, are encouraged to actively participate, allocate the necessary resources in time and budget, and convey the message that teachers are responsible for implementing classroom interventions with integrity (Rathvon, 2008).

TASK: Work through staff resistance to SEL implementation

- Build a relationship.
- Model an example.
- Provide evidence-based research for effectiveness.
- Ask a colleague to speak about its effectiveness.
- Get administrative support.
- Meet together to plan.
- Understand beliefs and motivations.
- Support teachers in acquiring new practices.

Support Request Form

A support request form can be used to introduce your role to educational stakeholders and let them know how you can support them.

COACHING REFLECTION FORM

This form is for educational stakeholders to review strategies in collaboration with an SEL coach or lead implementer.

Educator Name: _____ Strategy I would like to try: _____

Step One: Goal Setting

- What are the benefits of this strategy?

- What are the needs for change?

- Personal qualities that will help you deliver this strategy

- People who can help you

- Resources you need to help you

Notes:

Step Two: Reflections of Positive School Culture

- How will this strategy develop a positive school or classroom culture?

- How will you continue to remind yourself to schedule time to practice this strategy?

Notes:

Discuss the Above With Your SEL Coach or Lead Implementer

- Any needs uncovered?

- Any modifications that need to be made?

- How will this align with other strategies that I use to promote positive climate?

Notes:

Monitor the Effectiveness of the SEL Coach

How do we monitor the efficacy of the classroom/teacher and support/coaching conversations and approaches? Ask the staff to describe what they found effective or not to give a better understanding of how to tailor your coaching efforts in the future. Administrators may also want to participate in understanding what works. But they need to make sure that they are not explicitly asking why they wanted to work with the coach to maintain the confidentiality of their work together. If the teacher found it helpful, you may ask what specifically they did that helped. If the teacher did not find it helpful, you may ask in what way they could have approached it differently.

TASK: Measure effectiveness through a brief evaluation

Working With the SEL Coach:

What was your experience working with the SEL coach?

_____

_____

_____

What was helpful?

_____

_____

_____

What could you have used more of in the coaching collaboration? Is there a way that the SEL coach could have approached the work with you differently?

_____

_____

_____

ANNA LAIL

....

Social Emotional Learning Coach

Washington

1. *What did you find was most effective about the program or practice?*

    Right now, the most effective practices have more to do with teacher education and supports. Ongoing professional development is critical for implementation fidelity and success. In addition to educating the staff and teachers, universalizing SEL supports has been a critical piece of the practice.

2. *What did you find did not work during the program implementation?*

    Teacher buy-in is the most difficult part of program implementation; however, the pandemic placed SEL front and center, and so buy-in is increasing.

3. *What is the best way to increase schoolwide implementation of Social Emotional Learning in your experience?*

    Having a specialist in the building focused on driving supports and implementation is critical.

4. *What was your specific role and contributions in the SEL implementation process? What was the first thing you did?*

    I was the lead on putting supports into play for our building. The first thing that I began to work towards was coaching the adults and creating space for their own social and emotional needs. This included temperature checks and climate checks for the staff, in addition to working on supports for their individual classroom. Moving toward buildingwide implementation, with Social and Emotional Learning embedded throughout the day, requires buildings to look at discipline practices, classroom management, and the ways in which we view behavior.

5. *What were the key relationships that mattered most? What were the key sources of support or resistance you encountered?*

    Every building has teacher leaders and gaining their confidence in best practices was of great importance. These were key relationships to establish for implementation to be successful. "But this is the way we've always done it" and/or "I'm here to teach academics" are two ongoing places of resistance we are working through as a building team.

6. *What was most difficult or challenging?*

    The most difficult or challenging thing was the exhaustion of the teachers before asking them to try new things amidst a new virtual/hybrid learning experience.

7. *What were the skills you had to have to do the work of SEL implementation?*

   Personal SEL skills, in addition to paying attention to the latest trends in research.

8. *When you think of the future of Social Emotional Learning in your system or your work, what gives you a sense of hope? What makes you concerned or worried?*

   What gives me the most hope is the continued pursuit of the science behind SEL, most specifically, applied educational neuroscience. It removes the stigma of "soft skills" from the practice. What makes me most worried is the reality that for schools not engaging in SEL, the equity gap will continue to grow.

CHAPTER 9

....

ADVANCE YOUR PRACTICE

Communicator

The role of communicator is very important for the SEL coach. And it can involve so many different things. You may find that some of these things are part of your duties and others are not. Some things that SEL coaches may do within this role include writing a monthly newsletter, team-booster emails, having informal hallway conversations, and providing information on the website. It is appreciated when the SEL coach does a good job of including people who need to be in the loop. Communicating with staff about processes for one-on-one meetings, teaching lessons, and giving feedback after observations are vital. Coaches should provide follow-up and follow-through. And once given a direction, they should run with it and involve all stakeholders. They are an important key to getting buy-in and building momentum for the implementation process. Some coaches will present to PTSA and parenting events. Providing an all-staff weekly update but being sensitive to not sending out too many emails, hanging out in the staff lounge, and being there to offer support and strategies can be part of the SEL coach's role.

PHASE 1: COMMUNICATION ROLE TASKS

Areas of Communication

The communication skills include the ability to listen and be empathetic to all stakeholders and discuss problems and solutions effectively without becoming emotional. These skills are used in writing, speaking, and presenting to a variety of different groups and being able to assess their level of understanding and interest in the topic. The ability to be objective and communicate competently even when there are conflicting opinions is key.

Creating positive, supportive relationships between SEL coaches and teachers could lead to benefits for the students by decreasing burnout among teachers, allowing for better communication and teamwork.

Communications to parents should address these questions: Why is it good or beneficial for kids? Why do we (the school or district) find the intervention valuable? How is it (or could it be) making a difference in their lives? Most importantly, but often neglected, how can parents or guardians use this information at home? SEL coaches should inform parents about the power of common language between home and school. Potential barriers for stakeholders/parents could include lack of open communication, or difference in communication styles, and insensitivity of stakeholders. District information websites can be a barrier to clear and quick communication, which leads to parents being unsure how to navigate. Get in front of these barriers by checking the system, asking questions, and having a problem-solving process.

TASK: Create a communication flowchart to gauge areas of need

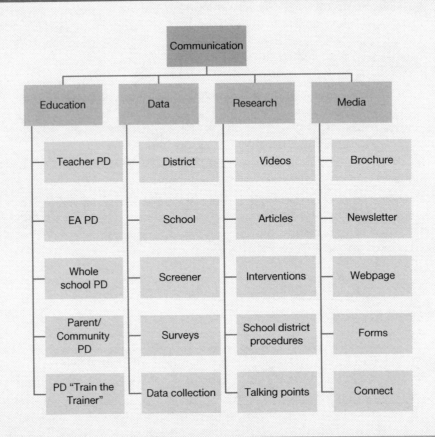

Collaboration: With Whom Have You Collaborated at Your School?

The SEL coach should be prepared to understand what all roles are in the system and how they work together. This includes understanding and communicating with principals, counselors, deans, teachers (both classroom and specials), special education teachers, school psychologists, educational assistants or paraprofessionals, ELL teachers, assistant principals, push-in therapists or counselors, office staff, SLP, OT/PT, literacy coach, before and after school club, school resource officers, and building leaders. Included below is an example at the elementary level but the process could be adapted for middle and high school as well.

TASK: Brainstorm collaboration partners: Who have you worked with and who should you try to work with?

Create a list of departments in your school. How have you worked with each of them? What are the results?

DEPARTMENT	HOW HAVE YOU COLLABORATED WITH THIS DEPARTMENT?	WHAT HAVE THE RESULTS LOOKED LIKE?
Kindergarten teachers		
First-grade teachers		
Second-grade teachers		
Third-grade teachers		
Fourth-grade teachers		
Fifth-grade teachers		
Special services teacher		
Mental health services		
Administrators		
Paraprofessionals/ Educational assistants		
Classified staff		
Other		

Levels of Communication

As a coach, you will need to consider how you are accessing the entire community that you serve. Communication will not only need to take place in team meetings, professional development, and coaching with individuals or small groups. It will also require written communication and alternative means to reach your educational stakeholders outside of the school building.

TASK: Determine ways to get the word out about SEL

1. Newsletters: A weekly or bimonthly newsletter can help to give stakeholders small pieces of information or reminders about what strategies they are working on and how they can access resources. It can be used to inform people about upcoming events as well. Staff can be reminded of how you can work with them: brainstorming session, modeling a lesson or strategy, observations, helping to develop relationships, and engagement strategies.

2. Blogs: Another way to discuss strategies and examples in the long form is to write a blog. A blog can be used to describe what you can do and cannot do in your role as a coach. You may also ask to be a guest host on the blogs that your teachers write. Provide additional strategies directly to the families through this well-established means.

3. Reports: Creating a report for educational stakeholders to describe how the coach is performing the different aspects of the job and what data is being collected about the system can be very helpful. It allows administrators to have discussions about how the coach is supporting the building. It will be helpful to acknowledge the gains that have been made both qualitatively and quantitatively due to the coach's work. This is especially needed if there are some misunderstandings and confusion about the coach role. The purpose is to help stakeholders understand more about the deliverables of the coach and to illuminate any questions. An action plan can further be developed with the feedback of those who read the report.

The purpose of your communications efforts is to make sure that we are providing our audience (parents, teachers, etc.) with evidence-based materials. SEL coaches need to be thoughtful about how the communication traverses the entire system. The role includes various levels of communication through education, data, research (gathering and disseminating materials), and media sources.

Selling the SEL Coach Role

In *Leading for Change Through Whole School Social Emotional Learning*, there is a section about creating a pitch for SEL to the system. In this book, I'd like to advance how coaches can pitch themselves to the educational stakeholders in your system. The pitch is designed to help explain what you do and why you do it to various levels.

The purpose is to create clarity by letting your educational stakeholders know what you do and why. Visibility is key. Having an elevator speech, research points, and brief stories to illustrate your mission in your back pocket will help when you are in situations where people don't understand what you do. If you aren't talking about it regularly, why should anyone else? The intervention or program should be visible on your website, in discussions at the district and school level, and in the community. This is part of a continual process of improvement toward your goals.

The pitch can include multiple types. The elevator speech would be 30 seconds or less. A 30-minute pitch is ideal for parents, families, and the community. A 2-hour pitch for SEL and your role would be helpful for administration and principals. And a full day would be for teachers or others who directly work with students.

TASK: Create a pitch for your work as the SEL coach

Example:

Who we are? We have our own unique skill sets and experience, but we are also questioners, listeners, problem-solvers, evidence-based practitioners, helpers, data collectors, classroom observers, interventionists, systems people, and trained.

Why do we do it? We are here to help our school and staff develop strategies to better our students' social and emotional skills, which will in turn help them academically and with their life skills.

What is your story that connects you to this work? Why do you think it is important? Adding a personal touch will help you to connect your work with the work of others.

Yearly Report

It is vital to communicate all we have done for our stakeholders, particularly the school board. You can model the report based on other successful programs. Or you can use the recommended structure of the report with the following sections: acknowledgments and partnerships, vision statement, describing SEL, history of the SEL intervention, terms and definitions, fidelity of implementation, using data to guide direction, sustainability and evaluation, key findings, and recommendations. This report can measure the impact on the school and system.

The purpose of your communications efforts is to make sure that we are providing our audience (parents, teachers, etc.) with evidence-based materials. You want to make your schedule public so it is easy to access you. SEL coaches need to be thoughtful about how the communication traverses the entire system. The role includes various levels of communication through education, data, research (gathering and disseminating materials), and media sources.

TASK: Include questions that inform the report (from the SEL coaches' perspective)

1. What direction is your school going with SEL implementation? What was their first step?

2. How many meetings have you been a part of?

3. With whom have you collaborated at your school?

4. What resources (videos, PPTs, articles, interventions) have you used at your school?

5. Have you done any observations? If so, what was the feedback process like after the intervention?

6. How many individual teacher meetings have you had?

7. What percentage of your day is used to provide Tier 1/Tier 2/Tier 3 interventions?

8. Have you demonstrated a model classroom?

9. How many professional development sessions have you held? What were the topics? Who was the audience?

10. Did you assess your staff's current level of beliefs and motivation around SEL?

11. Have you formed an SEL team? Who are the members and what are their roles in the system?

12. Are you a member of any other teams? What role do you play?

PHASE 2: COMMUNICATION ROLE TASKS

Engaging Parents and Families in the Work

Family engagement is critical. This includes frequent, regular contact with the school that is positive. There needs to be communication about what SEL means and how parents can participate in meaningful ways. This includes involvement as an equal partner, not just someone who contributes to the school financially. This is particularly important to think about how to meet the needs of ALL parents. There may be differences in language, communication styles, etc. Making families feel welcome is a priority, especially considering that some families have not had good experiences in their own schooling and that may influence the way in which they react to some things that happen in the school environment.

Communicating with parents could include creating a parent newsletter with action items that connect with the things you are working on in the school building. SEL coaches can learn more about the SEL competencies that students are struggling with at home and provide strategies to meet those needs. Another great strategy is to host parent workshops to introduce yourself, as the coach position will not be familiar with the role of SEL coach in the school. Make sure to continue to ask parents and the community about the school climate to inform decisions for parent programming.

TASK: Create a book club for families

Create an SEL book club that parents and families can participate in. These books can focus on ways to understand their own social and emotional competencies and those of their children. There may even be a book-sharing event where families can read a book with their child and discuss it with the book club group. It will be helpful in finding ways to practice social and emotional skills with their students.

A Parent/Family Network

Schools can educate their parents and families about Social Emotional Learning. These efforts may require extra time and resources, but they will provide families with a greater understanding of the skills involved with SEL. Education efforts can help to bring about greater parent involvement and understanding. It is important to include information about why SEL is good for kids, why schools find value in teaching SEL, how it can make a difference in their lives, and how families can use this information at home. Again, parents and families need to know what's in it for them.

TASK: Create a parent education team with a focus on your SEL efforts

Use the form from Chapter 4, Task: Inventory SEL general knowledge (page 44), to review what your parents and guardians know about SEL (shown as P/G). Check all the boxes that you believe stakeholders understand about Social Emotional Learning. Then for the ones that the team does not check, circle the areas that you think would be beneficial for them to know.

Parent/Guardian Workshop

The parent/family education team members will review current materials and consider these questions: What questions do we have? What gaps do we still need to cover? What are the ideas we have for parent engagement and activities and an overview of structure? How long will the presentation need to be?

Make something as a takeaway so the families can take notes and jot down ideas. Keep track of attendees and email addresses. Then you can send the families an exit ticket to hear more about what they learned, what they plan to use at home, and any additional questions or comments they may have.

TASK: Create an agenda for the workshop

1. Welcome to school, introduction to the coach, and description of the role

2. Define SEL

3. The vision of SEL for school and outcomes for children

4. Introduce teams who are working on this effort

5. SEL at home: Introduce one to three strategies that families can use at home

6. Questions (for a specific time)

Parent/Family Feedback

At the end of each presentation, the SEL coach should gather information about what was beneficial.

Here are some examples of what we learned from parents/families from past SEL workshops:

1. Cooperation creates more responsibility; growth mindset; telling isn't teaching: remind myself!

2. Focus on the positive behavior; make sure you recognize/apologize when not handling stuff well.

3. "Failure is OK": persevere, share own struggles.

4. Kids learn best when they are predictable, consistent, stable, and positive; they can follow step-by-step policy; take ownership, communicate after the conflict.

5. Provide personal examples of overcoming/persevering; EMPOWER kids: give them choices that will encourage them to achieve/accomplish/do on their own/try/work/complete.

It is important to learn what parents and families have to say about Social and Emotional Learning programs. This can be understood in interviews about the programming. But there are many things that need to happen before we can interview them. The first thing is to make them aware of the programming and the benefits of SEL. This can be done through family nights, where families and students can learn social and emotional competencies together in active projects or discussions. Talking to the families can help give us an understanding of how their children have benefitted from these programs and the ways that parents and families have benefitted as well.

TASK: Collect data from parent/family workshop to enhance future offerings

The easy three questions that can be asked after a parent workshop are:

- What did you learn that you would like to share?

- What do you plan to try at home?

- What questions do you have?

Create a data sheet with information from the exit ticket:

DATE	SCHOOL	WHAT DID YOU LEARN?	WHAT STRATEGY WOULD YOU LIKE TO TRY AT HOME?	ANY QUESTIONS ABOUT THE PRESENTATION?

PHASE 3: COMMUNICATION ROLE TASKS

Communication About Problem Areas

One area where the coach can be particularly helpful is to work with areas of confusion that the stakeholders have. The SEL coach can do the research and heavy lifting to interpret some of these things for the rest of the community.

They can be specific interventions by creating a more readable version. They can include processes for how to do classroom observations or other things like that. They can be figuring out how to navigate some of the political issues or understanding the perspectives of others who see the problems from a different vantage point or even things like motivation. For example, what does the research say about intrinsic versus extrinsic motivation? SEL coaches can talk about their work with specific groups in the school like literacy coaches or bring in work from outside trainings.

Ask administrators questions they may have about the role and try your best to answer them. The administrators may not have a clear understanding of what the SEL coach is meant to do. And when that is the case, they may ask the coach to do things that would not naturally fall in that role.

TASK: Prepare for questions administrators may ask

Here are some examples of the types of questions that they may ask:

1. As we move forward to screen, instruct, monitor, and assess growth, is there a plan for the curriculum/program to use in classrooms as teachers take SEL into the classroom? Each classroom will have different needs and teachers will require training.

2. How do we help teachers to understand this person's role and build capacity?

3. Is there any one-on-one work with students? If so, what are the criteria for such support?

4. Clarify the roles of different educational stakeholders including the SEL coach, counselor, behavior specialist, and so forth. How do the different roles fit together to meet student needs?

5. What should we expect from our SEL coach at the beginning of the year?

6. What PD will happen throughout the year, and is there an expectation that we give staff meeting or PD time for this new learning to be shared with the school teams?

7. How much time is going to be given to this topic this year?

8. What kind of curriculum support can we anticipate if our school is ready for it?

9. What will this person's daily schedule look like? What are the specific things they will do? What if there isn't a classroom need for coaching?

10. How will the SEL coach be evaluated?

11. How should we support these staff members in their new role?

12. Where should we house these new staff members?

13. Will there be some form of communication that will be rolled out to our parent community regarding this new stuff?

14. What is being communicated to the community regarding the plan?

15. What data will be kept monitoring the effectiveness of this program?

As you can see, in the beginning, without clarity, there will be a lot of questions. The ones that are listed above are just from administrators. The teachers, parents/families, and students will also have questions. That is why clarity is of the utmost importance. And when it cannot be clear because it is in transition, let the stakeholders know that too.

Communicating Recommendations

Asking for recommendations will help to determine the direction of your SEL implementation. Principals will be especially helpful in this effort. Principals can share the details of the training that was held at their buildings, the role of the SEL coach in supporting the implementation, their recommendations for the other schools, their successes, and suggestions for continued support. The task below includes examples from administrators about SEL implementation.

TASK: Understand recommendations from administrators and use them when possible

Key points and sample recommendations are noted below.

1. Schools should hold training of 45 to 90 minutes before the school year starts.

2. SEL coaches should demonstrate lessons in classrooms at all schools. This was received well by classroom teachers.

3. Another option that works is to train EAs or paraprofessionals, other classified staff, and parents.

4. The monthly assemblies were not implemented, and principals felt they were not needed.

(Continued)

(Continued)

5. Encourage teachers to use the SEL language throughout the day (integrate, use when lining students up at the door, etc.).

6. Encourage teachers to embed positive classroom management strategies.

7. Incorporate the "WHY" whenever possible.

8. Consider having an educational assistant or paraprofessional training during one of the training days. Include how to coach students through problem-solving.

The role of the communicator will look different in each system. It will be up to the SEL coach to understand the needs in their specific system.

Getting Testimonials From Teachers

One strategy that is effective is to have teachers talk about their positive experiences with SEL implementation, SEL curriculum, or work with the SEL coach. It can be helpful in demonstrating the positive experiences of teachers to encourage others to seek help from them. This can be done in several ways. It can be another way to help teachers buy in and want to invite their colleagues in joining them in practicing them. It will be important to get examples of how they found it useful.

TASK: Ask teachers what they find useful about SEL and any information they have about it

After you have asked the teachers what they find useful, determine if it is appropriate to talk to others about what they find useful. Ask permission to use their words. And determine how you can promote their testimony.

Some ideas:

- Newsletters

- Email

- Professional development

- Staff meetings

- Other communication mechanisms used by your school

PHASE 4: COMMUNICATION ROLE TASKS
Investing in Community Stakeholders

To educate the community, it might be useful to tie SEL to the concept of protective factors. Protective factors increase resilience and buffer students against the negative influence of risk factors. Some of the protective factors that overlap with Social Emotional Learning include social skills. Youth who are socially competent and engage in positive interpersonal relationships with their peers are less likely to participate in negative risk behaviors. Youth who interact with prosocial peers or those who are a positive influence are at a lower risk for engaging in problem behaviors. Let the community know about the work you are doing to positively impact the protective factors of students. Below is an example of what that might look like.

TASK: Create an information sheet that discusses protective factors

Increasing the protective factors for students

To celebrate how schools are promoting protective factors through SEL, demonstrate a few examples of what is happening at your school.

PROTECTIVE FACTOR	OUR SCHOOL	A FEW EXAMPLES
Social and emotional competence	Social Emotional Curriculum has been adopted in all schools in our district.	Riverside Elementary has been using a problem-solving process at recess that has been showing great success in managing altercations.
Early identification of externalizing and internalizing behaviors	Half of the district schools use the universal screener to identify students with externalizing and internalizing behaviors and develop a process to provide strategies and interventions for those students.	Potter Middle School determined how the SEL implementation pilot group saw a decrease in the number of externalizing behaviors exhibited by their students.

(Continued)

(Continued)

PROTECTIVE FACTOR	OUR SCHOOL	A FEW EXAMPLES
Positive relationships with adults	Having a supportive relationship with an adult is one of the most reported protective factors that contribute to resilience.	Park High School has used the "dot project" to identify students who do not have strong relationships with an adult at school and they match the teachers up with these students.
Self-regulation	Students in elementary school are taught self-regulation strategies in the selected curriculum.	South Ridge Elementary sends a home link to help families work on self-regulation skills at home. The principal reported that parents have talked about how their students use the problem-solving steps at home.

Advocating for Building Your Infrastructure: Promoting Community Understanding

Part of the role of the SEL coach is to promote understanding for the community. As we often do in education, we use jargon and acronyms as a shorthand and may not realize how our stakeholders need more descriptive language to know what we are talking about. SEL coaches can enhance their practice by doing things like writing a letter to the editor of their local paper.

TASK: Let your community know about your good work

Ideas to consider:

- Connect SEL with employability skills.

- Interview community leaders about specific social and emotional competencies and how they benefit their work.

- Discuss local needs and how they can be met through SEL.

- Interview students about what SEL means to them.

MICHELLE TRUJILLO

....

Author, Speaker, and Former Building Administrator

Nevada

Interview:

1. *What did you find was most effective about the program or practice?*

   I find it most effective to ensure that all adults within the system understand, practice, and model SEL themselves prior to teaching students SEL skills.

2. *What is the best way to increase schoolwide implementation of Social Emotional Learning in your experience?*

   In my opinion, the best way to increase schoolwide implementation is to begin with the educators. We must help them to know that practice precedes program. In my experience, I have found it imperative that adults within the educational system understand SEL as a way of being before they adopt a program or curriculum for school implementation. Although finding an evidence-based curriculum is crucial in the long run, often we receive funding with a deadline for expenditure. This can place pressure upon school leaders to choose a "program" without considering the demographics or needs of students and/or adults within the school community.

3. *What are the lessons you would pass on to other people in your role?*

   Investment is born in experience. We must help our educators to understand and practice SEL skills so that they can begin to see the benefits of nourishing our own well-being. When they experience the benefits, they are more likely to invest in teaching SEL in their classrooms and integrating SEL into the school culture.

4. *What were the skills you had to have to do the work of SEL implementation? Where and how did you learn those skills?*

   SEL skills! To authentically implement any promising program or practice, we must leverage our own Social Emotional Learning skills, and to do that we must nourish our own social emotional well-being. I created a framework for this that aligns with the SEL competencies as defined by the Collaborative for Academic, Social, and Emotional Learning (CASEL). The benefit of using this framework is that it

   (Continued)

(Continued)

considers the fact that educators currently have a great deal on their plates and, thus, do not need another thing to "do." What is helpful, however, is to consider the way in which we demonstrate social emotional competencies. Understanding and assessing our state of being in the context of being reflective, intentional, empathetic, connected, accountable, and equitable helps us, as educators, to consider how we already practice certain behaviors. When we reflect on our own strengths and recognize opportunities for growth within our own well-being, we are better prepared to practice the aligned SEL skills and teach these skills to our students.

CHAPTER 10

....

SUPPORT FOR COACHES

As previously mentioned, there will be ups and downs in this role. You may be faced with explaining your role many times. This is all to be expected with a new role and implementation. But at times, it can take a toll on the individual. In this chapter, we will go over some ideas for how to manage some of the stress related to being an SEL coach.

CREATE A PERSONAL MISSION STATEMENT

It will be helpful for you to find your why and create a personal mission statement for yourself. These will be important to have when things are difficult and you are struggling to find your footing. You can take time to reflect on what your purpose for taking the role was—what you hoped to help people do and what you wanted to learn about yourself.

Some examples of mission statements for yourself could be the following:

- As the SEL coach, I will facilitate students and the school community in creating and maintaining a positive school climate through professional development, coaching, modeling social and emotional competencies, and implementing SEL systemwide.

- As the SEL coach, I will collaborate with school staff and the community to create the scaffolding to support our students and the overall school climate.

- As the SEL coach, I will work to build capacity in the school site to improve student learning through climate, community, and staff empowerment.

In the beginning, you will want to be clear about the expectations of yourself in this new role and how others will perceive what you do. In those first weeks, you will want to meet with the principal as much as possible to talk about the role and ask about current policies. Ask lots of questions and listen deeply to try and understand the needs of your building. Begin crafting an initial presentation to staff, because how you introduce yourself will matter. Continue to educate yourself. There is so much to learn about people, policies, change processes, and the nuances of social and emotional skill adoption. Connect with as many people as possible, inside and outside your building, in roles like paraprofessionals and PTSA.

TYPES OF SUPPORT

Every school is designed differently with varying school staff. In large districts, there are often many levels of administration to manage the various programs. In rural districts, staff often wear multiple hats and are responsible for a variety of different things. In this new role, the SEL coach will need to have many types of support. First is to support yourselves by learning from your experiences, whether you use a formal process or just notes to yourself. Keep track of the things you have done well and can celebrate. This includes individual/school-specific accomplishments. Use specific action words to describe how you built, helped, created, modeled, worked, established, and collaborated. And keep track of the things you would like to improve next year (action plan for improvement). This can include personal skills (time management, organization, direction) as well as improved practice (specific knowledge and skills related to interventions) and how personal relationships were managed in this innovation and change process. Keeping a journal and writing for yourself can help to guide your reflection.

The SEL coach will need to set the table for uncertainty in this process. It will be important to seek out colleagues who "get it." Getting social support is crucial for all of us, particularly for someone who is trying to make change. Talk with people who see that it is worth the effort and perseverance to see it through. Social support can help you to bring joy and laughs to the work when possible. In fact, you should seek out people who make you laugh and bring you joy in and outside of the school building. You may even ask to observe a colleague or ask the colleague to observe you in your work to determine if there are any areas of growth. This level of collaboration can happen when there is trust and communication among your colleagues.

Your supervisor can be another source of support. Ideally, they will also "get it" and they can provide you with the support that you may need when you feel stuck. Regularly schedule meetings with this person, even if you think you won't need them. These check-ins will help your supervisor to understand more about you and your process and to determine if your approach is realistic. They can help you to see your situation through a more objective lens and can help to develop the necessary skills to take on the many different parts of this role. The onboarding process will provide the supervisor the time to teach new SEL coaches how are they integrated into the culture and what supports they have, and to provide training for new coaches while supporting the people who have been previously in the role. It is an ever-evolving process where you should be supported with your new learning every year.

GET FEEDBACK FROM PRINCIPALS

As you become more familiar with the expectations of your role, you will want to get some feedback from your principals. How do they see you embracing different parts of the role? What do they feel your strengths and challenges are? This type of feedback can be invaluable. And while you may not always agree with the things they are saying. It is important to understand the lens that they are looking through as far as the expectations they have for you in this role.

Ask the following questions:

1. Leadership/facilitator: Has your SEL coach been successful at getting to know the staff? Have they become a trusted source of information and support?

2. Teaming: Has the SEL coach been successful at establishing and/or maintaining a school-level team? Are the meetings productive and meaningful and have attainable goals?

3. Coach/training: How does your SEL coach work directly with staff to implement interventions? Where are their strengths? What is an area of growth? Has your coach been able to promote understanding of the program with the staff? What areas have they covered?

4. Data support: Has your SEL coach worked with data to inform the work at your school? What data have they used? How has it informed the decision-making process for your building?

5. Professional development: How has your SEL coach communicated information to teachers, parents, students, paraprofessionals, and administration? What is your experience with your coach providing professional development?

6. Communication: In what ways does your SEL coach communicate about the SEL intervention? Who have they spoken to? Are they able to be clear and consistent in their message to educational stakeholders?

PRIORITIZING COACHING SUPPORT
CHECKLIST FOR ADMINISTRATORS

This can help to communicate what you can do to support different areas in the role. Give this to your educational stakeholders, particularly those in leadership. Sometimes a checklist can help others to conceptualize the ways in which they can be helped.

COACHING SUPPORT CHECKLIST BY PRIORITY

Name: _____

School: _____

In each subcategory, prioritize your needs in order of importance related to your work.

How can the SEL coach support the building (1–10)?

☐ Teacher PD

☐ Staff PD (educational assistants or paraprofessionals, certificated, etc.)

☐ Survey administration and results

☐ SEL curriculum instruction and teaching

☐ Universal screener

☐ Identify current sources of data

☐ Assess needs for an electronic data-collection system

☐ Determine needed resources for implementation

☐ Self-care strategies

☐ Parent workshops

How can the SEL coach support the teachers (1–6)?

☐ Classroom observations

☐ Designing a PD

☐ Daily planning

☐ Collecting data

☐ Integrating SEL into daily routine

☐ Specific SEL strategies

CREATING BOUNDARIES AROUND THE WORK

The SEL coach must be able to establish boundaries. In this new role, they will have to learn how to put down former responsibilities in the building—for example, if they used to be a teacher or counselor in the building and have moved into the role of full-time SEL coach. They will have to train the others who have seen them in another role to do the same.

One thing that you must have clear communication about is your role in the building. The examples below have happened to other SEL coaches. One could make a case that there is some part of the SEL role in each of these activities. But if done regularly, they take away from the true intent of the role, which is to provide universal support for the SEL implementation. Talk with your administration about their thoughts and if these things would fall into your role. And if so, how can you advocate for "when needed" and not all the time?

Examples:

1. Supervision: Present during lunch and transitions to help students and be a visible adult to positively reinforce students doing the right thing and give reminders to students to demonstrate expectations.

2. Substitution: Cover the classroom if the teacher wants to see another teacher teach/model social and emotional competencies.

3. Helper: Step in to help in the classroom during the teacher crisis.

4. Discipline: Student discipline interventions as part of the administration team.

5. Goal setting: Meet with D/F students and assist them with goal setting.

6. Personal support: Provide personal support to the teachers and staff when they need it.

7. Mediator: Difficult situations between staff members to work through.

8. PBIS: Coordinating schoolwide reinforcement system.

9. After-school activities: A "Chess Club" to work with students around problem-solving strategies, strengthening perseverance, and adopting more of a growth mindset.

It is a valuable exercise to reflect on the ways that your boundaries have been crossed in the past. Do you find any patterns? Once you have achieved some clarity about the situations and individuals that stretch or break your boundaries, it is important to think about what sort of boundaries you need to create. You can establish boundaries by

1. Understanding your personal limits

2. Recognizing when feeling discomfort and resentment when asked to do something

3. Discussing your expectations directly

Building boundaries will take time and practice if this is something that you are not used to doing. And when you assert yourself for the first time, the people around you may find it a challenge. But continue to move forward in this work. Having boundaries can save you.

PERSONAL PLAN: THE OXYGEN MASK

This is worth repeating, as it was mentioned in *Leading for Change Through Whole School Social-Emotional Learning*. Most of us have experienced or seen a flight attendant give the speech that includes the guidance to put your oxygen mask on first before helping those around you. SEL coaches must have additional personal resources to deal with the unpredictability and stress of systems change. Self-care is a significant consideration and must be a planned event for implementers. Putting your oxygen mask on first is not selfish, it is essential (Rogers, 2019). One way to build resilience is to intentionally look for the good. When times are difficult, we need extra resources to keep us afloat. Training your mind to find the good in the day, the moment, or the person will help you shift your perspective. Keeping alert for the good things is a skill that pays to develop (Rogers, 2019).

SHIELD EXERCISE

This exercise might be helpful to prepare yourself for the SEL coach role. In each quadrant, write the following:

- Your strengths

- Your goals for this position

- Your non-negotiables or boundaries (e.g., won't work into the night or on weekends)

- Who is part of your support system

Place the shield somewhere that you can see it to remind you.

THE IMPORTANCE OF
SELF-COMPASSION AND SELF-CARE

Most people who get into education are trying to do the best they can for kids. For many of us, it is our way to help "change the world" and make a difference. The truth is that if you have made a difference to one person, you already have. But we educators are overachievers. Many of us have big hearts for these students. Their stories take a toll on us. And sometimes, educators suffer from vicarious or secondary trauma. This is the deterioration of our ability to empathetically respond to the pain and suffering of others. Educators who work with traumatized children can be vulnerable to secondary trauma. We bring it home with us. The signs include increased irritability or impatience, difficulty planning classroom activities and lessons, decreased concentration, denying that traumatic events impact students, feeling numb/detached, and/or intense feelings such as intrusive thoughts or dreams about students' trauma (Figley, 1995). That is why it is so important currently to invest in self-compassion and self-care. Self-compassion is the way you think about yourself. Self-care is the things you do (or don't do) for yourself. The work you do is so important, but you must take care of yourself. Take a moment to reflect on your own self-care and some of the effects that a lack of it or an emergence of secondary trauma can have on you.

Reflections on Your Practice: Self-Care

- What are my favorite things about being an SEL coach? If applicable, have they changed since my first year?

- Am I being challenged at an optimal level—new learning feels invigorating vs. overwhelming?

- Are the relationships that I have with my colleagues affirming? Do I seek them out to share good or bad news?

- Do my actions reflect my beliefs about students?

- What is the mindset that I go into staff meetings with?

- What things am I currently doing that I could remove or cut down and still meet the demands of my role?

- Do I have a good understanding of my priorities and make time to eliminate what is not a priority from my day?

- In what ways am I focusing on my own mental, emotional, and physical health every day?

- Am I excited to go to work today? What motivates me?

- Are my students excited to see me?

As you answer these questions, if you find that you are feeling less optimistic and more cynical, it may be time to invest in self-care.

CHECK IN ON YOURSELF

You may want to consider administering a questionnaire to yourself to determine if you are experiencing secondary traumatic stress. Some coaches will not be affected due to the positioning of their role in the system. But others will be affected due to the nature of systems change. Changing people's minds and hearts can be a grueling task. One assessment is the PROQOL (Professional Quality of Life), which can be accessed at www.proqol.org. There are other types of assessments that can gauge your level of self-care, self-compassion, resiliency, and burnout. It may be a good idea for you to administer one of these to yourself if you are struggling under the weight of this new role. And if you are feeling burned out or in need of self-care, commit to action to help yourself. This may include social support from friends and family or talking to your colleagues or a mental health professional.

ॐ ॐ ॐ

A FINAL WORD . . .

We are at an exciting time in education, where the pendulum swing is moving toward an understanding of the needs of a whole child. And we are recognizing the importance of relationships, engagement, and social and emotional competencies and their role in education. We are also learning that our educational stakeholders need more—more skills to deal with their own stressors and to help practice and model SEL with their students.

And you are lucky enough to be called SEL coach, so you get to be on the leading edge of this movement. You are a part of this shift in thinking. You can help our educators develop the competencies that can improve the lives of students. And that is a powerful and meaningful charge. You got this, SEL coach! Go change the world, one competency at a time.

REFERENCES

Allbright, T., Marsh, J., Kennedy, K., Hough, H., & McKibben, S. (2019). Social-emotional learning practices: Insights from outlier schools. *Journal of Research in Innovative Teaching & Learning, 12*(1), 35–52. https://doi.org/10.1108/JRIT-02-2019-0020

Bambaeeroo, F., & Shokrpour, N. (2017). The impact of the teachers' non-verbal communication on success in teaching. *Journal of Advances in Medical Education & Professionalism, 5*(2), 51–59.

Brackett, M., Bailey, C., Hoffman, J., & Simmons, D. (2019). RULER: A theory driven, systemic approach to social, emotional, and academic learning. *Educational Psychologist, 54*(3), 144–161. https://doi.org/10.1080/00461520.2019.1614447

Brackett, M., Patti, J., Stern, R., Rivers, S., Elbertson, N., Chisholm, C., & Salovey, P. (2009). A sustainable, skill-based model to building emotionally literate schools. In R. Thompson, M. Hughes, & J. Terrell (Eds.), *Handbook of developing emotional and social intelligence: Best practices, case studies, and tools* (pp. 329–358). Wiley.

Centers for Disease Control and Prevention. (2019). *A guide to evaluating professional development*. U.S. Department of Health and Human Services.

Centola, D. (2021). *Change: How to make big things happen*. Little, Brown Spark.

Cervone, B., & Cushman, K. (2012). *Teachers at work—Six exemplars of everyday practice: The students at the center series*. Jobs of the Future.

Coffey, J., & Horner, R. (2012). The sustainability of schoolwide positive behavior interventions and supports. *Exceptional Children, 78*(4), 407–422.

Collie, R., Shapka, J., & Perry, N. (2012). School climate and social-emotional learning: Predicting teacher stress, job satisfaction, and teaching efficacy. *Journal of Educational Psychology, 104*(4), 1189–1204.

Cook, C., Lyon, A., Kubergovic, D., Browning Wright, D., & Zhang, Y. (2015). A supportive beliefs intervention to facilitate the implementation of evidence-based practices within a multi-tiered system of supports. *School Mental Health, 7*, 49–60. https://doi.org/10.1007/s12310-014-9139-3

Cook, C., Volpe, R., & Livanis, A. (2010). Constructing a roadmap for future universal screening research beyond academics. *Assessment for Effective Intervention, 35*(4), 197–205.

Durlak, J., & DuPre, E. (2008). Implementation matters: A review of research on the influence of implementation on program outcomes and the factors affecting implementation. *American Journal of Community Psychology, 41*, 327–350. https://doi.org/10.1007/s10464-008-9165-0

Durlak, J., Weissberg, R., Dymnicki, A., Taylor, R., & Schellinger, K. (2011). The impact of enhancing students' social and emotional learning: A meta-analysis of school-based universal interventions. *Child Development, 82*(1), 405–432.

Elbertson, N., Brackett, M., & Weissberg, R. (2010). School-based social and emotional learning (SEL) programming: Current perspectives. In A. Hargreaves, A. Lieberman, M. Fullan, & D. Hopkins (Eds.), *Second international handbook of educational change* (Vol. 23, pp. 1017–1032). Springer. https://doi.org/10.1007/978-90-481-2660-6_57

Figley, C., ed. (1995). *Compassion fatigue: Coping with secondary traumatic stress disorder in those who treat the traumatized.* Brunner-Routledge.

Fineberg, H. (2014, April 8). *The paradox of disease prevention: Celebrated in principle, resisted in practice.* Institute of Medicine of the National Academies.

Greer, J., & Wethered, C. (1984). Learned helplessness: A piece of the burnout puzzle. *Exceptional Children, 50*(6), 524–530.

Gusky, T. (1988). Teacher efficacy, self-concept, and attitudes toward the implementation of instructional innovation. *Teacher and Teaching Education, 4*(1), 63–69. https://doi.org/10.1016/0742-051X(88)90025-X

Hall, P., & Simeral, A. (2008). *Building teachers' capacity for success: A collaborative approach for coaches and school leaders.* Association for Supervision and Curriculum Development.

Hamilton, L., Gross, B., Adams, D., Pilcher Bradshaw, C., Cantor, P., Gurwitch, R., Jagers, R., Murray, V. M., & Wong, M. (2021). *How has the pandemic affected students' social-emotional well-being? A review of the evidence to date.* CRPE.

Hamre, B., & Pianta, R. (2006). Student-teacher relationships. In G. Bear & K. Minke (Eds.), *Children's needs III: Development, prevention and intervention* (pp. 49–59). National Association of School Psychologists.

Herman, K., Reinke, W., & Thompson, A. (2020). Prevention science as a platform for solving major societal problems and improving population health. *Journal of Prevention and Health Promotion, 1*(1), 131–151. https://doi.org/10.1177/2632077020948786

Jagers, R., Rivas-Drake, D., & Borowski, T. (2018). *Equity & social and emotional learning: A cultural analysis.* CASEL.

Jennings, P., & Greenberg, M. (2009). The prosocial classroom: Teachers social and emotional competence in relation to student and classroom outcomes. *Review of Educational Research, 79*(1), 491–525. https://doi.org/10.3102/0034654308325693

Jones, S., Bailey, R., Kahn, J., & Barnes, S. (2019, April 30). Social-emotional learning: What it is, what it isn't, and what we know. *Education Next, 21*(4). https://educationnext.org/social-emotional-learning-isnt-know/

Joyce, B., & Showers, B. (2002). *Student achievement through staff development.* Association for Supervision and Curriculum Development.

Kofman, F. (2014). *Authentic communication: Transforming difficult conversations in the workplace.* Sounds True.

Leff, S., Thomas, D. E., Shapiro, E., Paskewich, B., Wilson, K., Necowitz-Hoffman, B., & Jawad, A. (2011). Developing and validating a new classroom climate observation assessment tool. *Journal of School Violence, 10,* 165–184. https://doi.org/10.1080/15388220.2010.539167

Levin, S., & Bradley, K. (2019). *Understanding and addressing principal turnover: A review of the research.* National Association of Secondary School Principals.

Mahfouz, J., Greenberg, M., & Rodriguez, A. (2019). *Principals' social and emotional competence: A key factor in creating caring schools.* Edna Bennett Pierce Prevention Research Center, Pennsylvania State University.

March, A., & Gaunt, B. (2013). *Systems coaching: A model for building capacity.* Florida Department of Education.

Marzano, R., Marzano, J., & Pickering, D. (2003). *Classroom management that works: Research-based strategies for every teacher.* Association for Supervision and Curriculum Development.

Patton, M. (2003). *Qualitative evaluation checklist.* Evaluation Checklists Project. www.wmich.edu/evalctr/checklists

Rathvon, N. (2008). *Effective school interventions.* Guilford Press.

Reyes, M., Brackett, M., Rivers, S., Elbertson, N., & Salovey, P. (2012). The interaction effects of program training, dosage, and implementation quality on targeted student outcomes for the RULER approach to social and emotional learning. *School Psychology Review, 41*(1), 82–99. https://doi.org/10.1080/02796015.2012.12087377

Rogers, J. (2019). *Leading for change through whole school social emotional learning: Strategies to build a positive school culture.* Corwin.

Simmons, D. N., Bracket, M., & Adler, N. (2018). *Applying an equity lens to social, emotional, and academic development*. Edna Bennett Pierce Prevention Research.

Sweeney, D. (2011). *Student-centered coaching: A guide for K–8 coaches and principals*. Corwin.

Taylor, R., Oberle, E., Durlak, J., & Weissberg, R. (2017). Promoting positive youth development through school-based social and emotional learning interventions: A meta-analysis of follow-up effects. *Child Development, 4,* 11–56. https://doi.org/10.1111/cdev.12864

Yoder, N. (2014a). *Self-assessing social and emotional instruction and competencies: A tool for teachers*. American Institutes of Research.

Yoder, N. (2014b). *Teaching the whole child: Instructional practices that support social-emotional learning in three teacher evaluation frameworks*. American Institutes for Research.

Zins, J., & Erchul, W. (2002). Best practices in school consultation. In A. Thomas & J. Grimes (Eds.), *Best practices in school psychology* (Vol. 1, pp. 625–643). National Association of School Psychologists.

INDEX

A SAGE Publishing Company

Helping educators make the greatest impact

CORWIN HAS ONE MISSION: to enhance education through intentional professional learning.

We build long-term relationships with our authors, educators, clients, and associations who partner with us to develop and continuously improve the best evidence-based practices that establish and support lifelong learning.

Keep learning...

Also from Jennifer E. Rogers

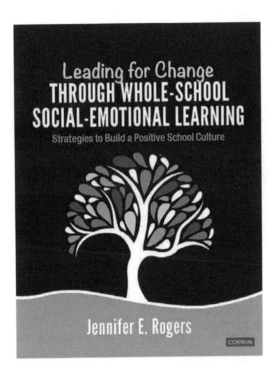

LEADING FOR CHANGE THROUGH WHOLE-SCHOOL SOCIAL-EMOTIONAL LEARNING

Strategies to Build a Positive School Culture

This book offers the support, strategies, processes, and tools to teach students SEL competencies in a comprehensive and sustainable way. The practical framework outlined in this book comprises real-world experiences and evidence-based strategies to integrate systemic change toward a positive school culture.

PROFESSIONAL DEVELOPMENT AND CONSULTING AVAILABLE

Rogers Training Solutions

Let Jennifer help you with effective, easy-to-use strategies to get your staff engaged in SEL implementation for ALL students. Rogers Training Solutions provides you with practical and research-based strategies to support YOU and your school or district in SEL implementation.

Visit **rogerstrainingsolutions.com** for information about consulting and additional resources.

Made in the USA
Monee, IL
06 June 2023

35353943R10129